Hard Press

Contents

This book is the result of a determination on my part to complete Mr. Hubbard's unfinished work, and having done this to set before the public a plain statement, not only of my own journey, but of his as well. For this reason I have included the greater part of Mr. Hubbard's diary, which he kept during the trip, and which it will be seen is published exactly as he wrote it, and also George Elson's account of the last few days together, and his own subsequent efforts.

I hope that this may go some way towards correcting misleading accounts of Mr. Hubbard's expedition, which have appeared elsewhere. It is due also to the memory of my husband that I should here put on record the fact that my journey with its results—geographical and otherwise—is the only one over this region recognised by the geographical authorities of America and Europe.

The map which is found accompanying this account of the two journeys sets forth the work I was able to accomplish. It does not claim to be other than purely pioneer work. I took no observations for longitude, but obtained a few for latitude, which served as guiding points in making my map. The controlling points of my journey [Northwest River post, Lake Michikamau and its outlet, and the mouth of the George River] were already astronomically fixed.

The route map of the first Hubbard Expedition is from one drawn for me by George Elson, with the few observations for latitude recorded by Mr. Hubbard in his diary as guiding points. My husband's maps, together with other field notes and records, I have not had access to, as these have never been handed over to me.

Grateful acknowledgment is here made of my indebtedness to Mr. Herbert L. Bridgman and Mr. Harold T. Ellis for their help and counsel in my work.

Here, too, I would express my sincere appreciation of the contribution to the book from Mr. Cabot, who, descendent of the ancient explorers, is peculiarly well fitted to speak of Labrador. The great peninsula has been, as he terms it, his "playground," and by canoe in summer or on snowshoes in winter he has travelled thousands of miles in the interior, thus placing himself in closest touch with it.

To Dr. Cluny Macpherson for his generous service I am deeply grateful.

To George Elson for his loyal devotion to Mr. Hubbard and myself my debt of gratitude must ever remain unpaid.

To Dr. James E. C. Sawyer, my beloved pastor, I am indebted for the title of my book.

MINA BENSON HUBBARD

CONTENTS

I. LEONIDAS HUBBARD, JR.
II. SLIPPING AWAY INTO THE WILDERNESS
III. CLIMBING THE RAPIDS
IV. DISASTER WHICH THREATENED DEFEAT
V. TO THE BEND OF THE RIVER
VI. CROSS COUNTRY TO SEAL LAKE WATERS
VII. OFF FOR MICHIRAMAU
VIII. SCARING THE GUIDES
IX. MOUNT HUBBARD AND WINDBOUND LAKE
X. MICHIKAMAU
XI. STORM-BOUND ON MICHIKAMATS
XII. THE MIGRATING CARIBOU
XII. ACROSS THE DIVIDE
XIV. THROUGH THE LAKES OF THE UPPER GEORGE
XV. THE MONTAGNAIS INDIANS
XVI. THE BARREN GROUND PEOPLE
XVII. THE RACE FOR UNGAVA
XVIII. THE RECKONING
DIARY OF LEONIDAS HUBBARD, JR.
NARRATIVE BY GEORGE ELSON

LIST OF ILLUSTRATIONS

The Author
Leonidas Hubbard, Jr.
Where Romance Lingers
Deep Ancient Valleys
George Elson
Job
Gilbert
On Into the Wilderness
The Fierce Nascaupee
The White Man's Burden
Making Canoe Poles
Job Was in His Element
Coming Down the Trail with Packs
Washing-Day
On the Trail
In the Heart of the Wilderness
Solitude (Seal Lake)
Joe
Skinning the Caribou
The Fall
Wild Maid Marion
Gertrude Falls
Breakfast on Michikamau
Stormbound
From an Indian Grave
A Bit of the Caribou Country
The Indians' Cache
Bridgman Mountains
The Camp on the Hill
A Montagnais Type
The Montagnais Boy
Nascaupees in Skin Dress
Indian Women and Their Rome
With the Nascaupee Women
The Nascaupee Chief and Men
Nascaupee Little Folk
A North Country Mother and Her Little Ones
Shooting the Rapids,
The Arrival at Ungava
A Bit of the Coast
A Rainy Camp
Working Up Shallow Water
Drying Caribou Meat and Mixing Bannocks
Great Michikamau
Carrying the Canoe Up the Hill on the Portage
Launching

4

In the Nascaupee Valley
A Rough Country
The French Post at Northwest River
Hudson's Bay Company Post as Northwest River
Night-Gloom Gathers
Map of Eastern Labrador showing Route

CHAPTER I

Leonidas Hubbard, Jr.

There was an unusual excitement and interest in Mr. Hubbard's face when he came home one evening in January of 1903.

We had just seated ourselves at the dinner-table, when leaning forward he handed me a letter to read. It contained the very pleasing information that we were shortly to receive a, for us, rather large sum of money. It was good news, but it did not quite account for Mr. Hubbard's present state of mind, and I looked up enquiringly.

"You see, Wife, it means that I can take my Labrador trip whether anyone sends me or not," he said triumphantly.

His eyes glowed and darkened and in his voice was the ring of a great enthusiasm, for he had seen a Vision, and this trip was a vital part of his dream.

The dream had begun years ago, when a boy lay out under the apple trees of a quiet farm in Southern Michigan with elbows resting on the pages of an old school geography, chin in palms and feet in air. The book was open at the map of Canada, and there on the other page were pictures of Indians dressed in skins with war bonnets on their heads; pictures of white hunters also dressed in skins, paddling bark canoes; winter pictures of dog-teams and sledges, the driver on his snow-shoes, his long whip in hand. The boy would have given all the arrow-heads he had for just one look at what he saw pictured there.

He was born, this boy, of generations of pioneer ancestors, the line of his mother's side running back to Flanders of three hundred years ago, through Michael Paulus Van Der Voort, who came to America from Dendermonde, East Flanders, and whose marriage on 18th November, 1640, to Marie Rappelyea, was the fifth recorded marriage in New Amsterdam, now New York. A branch runs back in England to John Rogers the martyr. It is the boast of this family that none of the blood has ever been known to "show the white feather." Among those ancestors of recent date of whose deeds he was specially proud, were the great-grandfather, Samuel Rogers, a pioneer preacher of the Church of Christ among the early settlers of Kentucky and Missouri, and the Grandfather Hubbard who took his part in the Indian fights of Ohio's early history. On both mother's and father's side is a record of brave, high-hearted, clean-living men and women, strong in Christian faith, lovers of nature, all of them, and thus partakers in rich measure of that which ennobles life.

The father, Leonidas Hubbard, had come "'cross country" from Deerfield, Ohio, with gun on shoulder, when Michigan was still a wilderness, and had chosen this site for his future home. He had taught in a school for a time in his young manhood; but the call of the out-of-doors was too strong, and forth he went again. When the

7

responsibilities of life made it necessary for him to limit his wanderings he had halted here; and here on July 12th, 1872, the son Leonidas Hubbard, Jr., was born.

He began by taking things very much to heart, joys and sorrows alike. In his play he was always setting himself some unaccomplishable task, and then flying into a rage because he could not do it. The first great trouble came with the advent of a baby sister who, some foolish one told him, would steal from him his mother's heart. Passionately he implored a big cousin to "take that little baby out and chop its head off."

Later he found it all a mistake, that his mother's heart was still his own, and so he was reconciled.

From earliest recollection he had listened with wide eyes through winter evenings, while over a pan of baldwin apples his father talked with some neighbour who had dropped in, of the early days when they had hunted deer and wolves and wild turkeys over this country where were now the thrifty Michigan farms. There were, too, his father's stories of his own adventures as hunter and miner in the mountains of the West.

It seemed to him the time would never come when he would be big enough to hunt and trap and travel through the forests as his father had done. He grew so slowly; but the years did pass, and at last one day the boy almost died of gladness when his father told him he was big enough now to learn to trap, and that he should have a lesson tomorrow. It was the first great overwhelming joy.

There was also a first great crime.

While waiting for this happy time to come he had learned to do other things, among them to throw stones. It was necessary, however, to be careful what was aimed at. The birds made tempting marks; but song-birds were sacred things, and temptation had to be resisted.

One day while he played in the yard with his little sister, resentment having turned to devotion, a wren flew down to the wood pile and began its song. It happened at that very moment he had a stone in his hand. He didn't quite have time to think before the stone was gone and the bird dropped dead. Dumb with horror the two gazed at each other. Beyond doubt all he could now expect was to go straight to torment. After one long look they turned and walked silently away in opposite directions. Never afterwards did they mention the incident to each other.

A new life began for him with his trapping. He learned to fish as well, for besides being a hunter, his father was an angler of State-wide reputation. The days on which his father accompanied him along the banks of the St. Joe, or to some more distant stream, were very specially happy ones. His cup was quite filled full when, on the day he was twelve years old, a rifle all his own was placed in his hands. Father and son then hunted together.

While thus growing intimate with the living things of the woods and streams, his question was not so much "What?" as "Why?" As reading came to take a larger part in life and interest to reach out to human beings, again his question was "Why?" So when other heroes took their places beside his father for their share of homage, they were loved and honoured for that which prompted their achievements more than for the deeds themselves.

Passionately fond of history, with its natural accompaniment geography, he revelled, as does every normal boy, in stories of the wars, Indian stories and tales of travel and adventure. His imagination kindled by what he had read, and the oft-repeated tales of frontier life in which the courage, endurance, and high honour of his own pioneer forefathers stood out strong and clear, it was but natural that the boy under the apple trees should feel romance in every bit of forest, every stream; that his thoughts should be reaching towards the out-of-the-way places of the earth where life was still that of the pioneer with the untamed wilderness lying across his path, and on into the wilderness itself.

Though born with all the instincts of the hunter, he was born also with an exquisitely tender and sympathetic nature, which made him do strange things for a boy.

One day a toad hopped into the beeyard and his father was about to kill it. The boy petitioned for its life and carried it away. It came back. Again it was carried away. Again it returned and this time was taken clear to the river.

Once a much loved aunt came to visit at his home bringing the little sister a beautiful, new doll. That night she trotted off to bed hugging the new treasure close. The boy did not love dolls; but when he saw the old, rag baby left lonely and forsaken be quietly picked it up and carried it to bed with him.

Years afterwards, when on a canoe trip on the Moose River, a disconsolate looking little Indian dog came and sat shyly watching us while we broke camp. We learned that the Indian owners had gone to the bush leaving him to fare as he might through the coming winter. When our canoe pushed out into the river there was an extra passenger. We brought him home to Congers, where he immediately carried consternation into the neighbouring chicken yards, convinced that he had found the finest partridge country on earth.

When sixteen the boy went to attend the Angola (Indiana) Normal School. Here his decision for Christ was made. He was baptized and united with the Church of Christ. Three years later his teaching took him to Northern Michigan where be found a wider range than he had yet known, and in the great pine forests of that country he did his first real exploring. Here were clear, cold streams with their trout and grayling, and here, when his work admitted, he hunted and fished and dreamed out his plans, his thoughts turning ever more insistently to the big, outside world where his heroes did their work.

He entered the University of Michigan, Ann Arbor, in 1893. High strung and sensitive, with a driving energy and ambition to have part in the larger work of the world, he suffered during the early part of his course all the agonies that come to those of such a nature while they grope in the dark for that which they are fitted to do. He reached out in many directions in his effort to provide the needful money to enable him to take his course, but without a sense of special fitness in any. It came however with his earliest attempts in journalistic work. The discovery with its measure of self-recognition brought a thrill that compensated for all the dark hours. He now felt assured of success.

His life in the University was one of varied and unceasing activity. In his studies history, literature, psychology claimed his special interest. He was an enthusiast in athletics, and found his field in running and boxing. The contest was as the wine of life to him. He was active in the literary and debating societies, and prominent in the Student's Christian Association, attending and taking part in the work of the local branch of the Church of Christ. His first newspaper work was done as an amateur on the college press. Then came assignments from the local dailies and correspondence for the Detroit papers.

He possessed the "news sense" to an unusual degree, delighting to take "beats" from under the very feet of his brother reporters.

In 1897 while he was still in Ann Arbor, just before Dr. James B. Angell, President of the University, left on his mission to Turkey, a telegram came from a Detroit evening paper directing him to see Dr. Angell and ask why he had changed his date of sailing.

Dr. Angell was not in the habit of telling reporters what he did not wish them to know, and when asked the question replied: "Haven't a word to say. I really don't know anything new at all." Then with a smile which he fondly believed to be inscrutable, he remarked: "Why, I don't even know whether I'll go to Turkey or not."

A few minutes later those last words of the President were reported over the wires, without the sarcasm and without the smile. That very evening, in big headlines on the first page, it was announced that there was some hitch, and that President Angell might not go as Minister to the Court of the Sultan.

The correspondents of the morning papers hastened to see President Angell, who insisted that if he had made such a remark it was in fun. But it was unavailing. The despatch had stirred up the officials in Washington, and the morning papers that printed the President's explanation printed over it the official statement, that the Porte was objecting to Dr. Angell, on account of his close relationship with the Congregational Missionary Board.

10

After his graduation in 1897, he took a position on the staff of a Detroit evening paper. Much of the two years of his newspaper work there was spent in Lansing covering State politics. In this line of work lay his chief interest, though he by no means confined himself to it.

His work made it possible for him to indulge his bent for dipping into the by-ways of human life. Utterly fearless, resolute, persistent, there was yet in his manner a beautiful simplicity, a gentleness and interest that rarely failed to disarm and win admission where he desired to enter. Added to this equipment were a fine sense of humour, a subtle sympathy, and a passionate tenderness for anyone or anything lonely or neglected or in trouble. So, as only the few do, he learned "Why."

Here amidst the struggles and temptations, the joys and disappointments, the successes and mistakes of his busy life, one hero rose surely to a place above all others, a place that was never usurped—"the man, Christ Jesus," worshipped in the years that were left, not only as the Redeemer of the world, but as his ideal hero.

This was his manliest man, so grandly strong and brave, yet so inexpressibly sweet-spirited and gentle, with a great human heart that, understanding so wholly, was yet so little understood; that in the midst of overwhelming work and care and loneliness hungered for human love and sympathy, giving so generously of its own great store, receiving so little in return. Here he found the strong purpose, the indomitable will, the courage that, accepting the hard things of life, could yet go unfalteringly forward, to the accomplishment of a great work, even though there was ever before Him the consciousness that at the end must come the great sacrifice.

In 1899 he decided to launch out into the wider field, which journalistic work in the East offered, and in the summer of that year he came to New York. Many were the predictions of brother reporters and friends that he would starve in the great city. It was a struggle. He knew no one, had letters to no one, but that was rather as he wished it than otherwise. He liked to test his own fitness. It meant risk, but he knew his own capabilities and believed in his own resourcefulness. He had thoroughly convinced himself that the men who achieve are those who do what other men are afraid to do. The difficulty would be to get an opening. That done, he had no fear of what would follow.

He began his quest with a capital of less than five dollars. There were many disappointments, much weariness, and a long fast which came near to persuading him that his friends' predictions were perhaps about to be fulfilled. *But he got his opening.*

Staggering with weakness, he had lived for two days in momentary dread of arrest for drunkenness. Then just when it seemed that he could go no farther, a former acquaintance from the West, of whose presence in the city he was aware, met him. Among the first questions was: "Do you need money?" and forthwith a generous fifteen dollars was placed in his hand. That day one of his special stories was

11

accepted, and only a few days later he was taken on the staff of the *Daily News*, where soon the best assignments of the paper were given him.

Do you know why you are getting the best work to do here?" asked one of the new friends.

"Why?"

"It's because you're *white*."

This position he retained until May of the following year, meantime contributing to the editorial page of *The Saturday Evening Post*. Then an attack of typhoid lost him his position; but he had made loyal friends, who delighted to come to his aid. Something of the quality of his own loyalty is expressed in an entry in his diary shortly after leaving the hospital. "Many good lessons in human nature. Learned much about who are the real friends, who may be trusted *to a finish*, who are not *quitters*, but it shall not be written." During the period of his convalescence which he spent among the Shawangunk Mountains of Sullivan County, New York, he decided that if it were possible he would not go back to newspaper work. A friend had sent him a letter of introduction to the editor of *Outing*, which in August he presented, and was asked to bring in an article on the preservation of the Adirondack Park as a national playground. The article proved acceptable, and thenceforth most of his work was done for that magazine.

In September he wrote his friend, Mr. James A. Leroy.

"*My Dear Jim,*—I think that regardless of your frightful neglect I shall be obliged to write you another note expressing sense of under-obligationness to you for that letter. It is the best thing I've run up against so to speak. As a result of it I am to have the pleasure of hastening Detroitward. There I shall register at the House. I shall sit in the window with my feet higher than my head, and wear a one-hundred-and-fifty-dollar-a-week air of nonchalance. When the festive Detroit reporter shys past looking hungrily at the cafe, I'll look at my watch with a wonder-if-it's-time-to-dress-for-dinner air and fill his soul with envy. This has been the dream that has haunted me ever since those childhood days when you and I ate at Spaghetti's and then went to the House to talk it over. I shall carry out the dire scheme and then—well, then, if Fate says for me to hustle across the Great Divide, I'll go with the feeling that life has not been in vain."

Later, January 14th of the following year, to the same friend who was then in Manila as secretary to Dean Worcester.

"You may think it wondrous strange that I should be here in Canada in mid-winter when I could as well be south. There is a mystery, and since you are on the other side of the world I don't mind telling. I am here on a filibustering expedition. I made a firm resolution some months ago that a certain portion of Canada should be annexed to the United States. I am here fostering annexation sentiment, and have succeeded so well that the consent is unanimous, and the annexation will occur just as soon as L. H., junior, is able to pay board for two, which will probably be a matter of a few weeks. So don't be surprised if you receive a square envelope containing an announcement which reads something like this:

```
Mr. and Mrs. _____
of Bewdley, Ontario,
announce the _____ of their daughter
_____
to
Mr. Leonidas Hubbard, Jr.
```

On his return to New York, a short time later, he was assigned a trip through the Southern States. Hence a telegram, on January 29th, to a quiet Canadian town. On January 31st a quiet wedding in a little church in New York, and then five months in the mountains of Virginia, North Carolina, Tennessee, and among the forests and cotton plantations of Mississippi.

Besides the work done for the magazine on this trip, he gave the *Atlantic Monthly* two articles, "The Moonshiner at Home," and "Barataria: The Ruins of a Pirate Kingdom."

During the fall, winter and early spring, our home was in Wurtsboro, Sullivan County, New York, a quaint old village in the beautiful Mamakating valley. Here he hunted and fished and worked, February found him on a snowshoe trip in Northern Quebec with the Montagnais Indian trappers, the outcome of which was his "Children of the Bush."

On April 1st, 1902, he entered the office as assistant editor of *Outing*. Here was a new field and another opportunity for testing his fitness. He threw himself into the work with characteristic energy and enthusiasm, and his influence on the magazine was marked from the first. He soon succeeded in projecting into it something of his own passionately human personality. In the fall of that year a noted angler commented to him on the change in it and his responsibility.

"When a big salmon comes to the top, there is a great swirl on the water. You don't see the salmon, but you know he is there," he said.

Office work left little time for writing; but in the early autumn of that year a vacation trip to the north shore of Lake Superior gave him two articles, "Where Romance Lingers," and "Off Days on Superior's North Shore."

In January 1903 the trip to Labrador was decided on, and his preparation for it begun. Before the winter was over his plans were made. On May 13th it was arranged with the magazine that it should go as an Outing expedition. The

13

preparation held for him the many difficulties and trials common to such undertakings, but also, perhaps, more than the usual pleasures.

The big map of Labrador looked back from the wall of the little study in Congers. We stood before it a long time discussing plans and possibilities. Then an eager, happy face was turned to me as he told how he would write the story and how he would have grown when he came home again.

On June 20th he sailed from New York with his little party.

In January following came that short message, "Mr. Hubbard died October 18th in the interior of Labrador."

In March were received the letters containing that final record of his life, which took from the hearts of those who loved him best the intolerable bitterness, because it told that he had not only dreamed his dream—*he had attained his Vision.*

It was a short, full life journey, and a joyous, undaunted heart that traversed it. Almost the most beautiful of its attributes was the joyousness.

He was "glad of Life because it gave him a chance to love and to work and to play."

He never failed to "look up at the stars."

He thought "every day of Christ."

Sometimes towards evening in dreary November, when the clouds hang heavy and low, covering all the sky, and the hills are solemn and sombre, and the wind is cold, and the lake black and sullen, a break in the dark veil lets through a splash of glorious sunshine. It is so very beautiful as it falls into the gloom that your breath draws in quick and you watch it with a thrill. Then you see that it moves towards you. All at once you are in the midst of it, it is falling round you and seems to have paused as if it meant to stay with you and go no farther.

While you revel in this wonderful light that has stopped to enfold you, suddenly it is not falling round you any more, and you see it moving steadily on again, out over the marsh with its bordering evergreens, touching with beauty every place it falls upon, forward up the valley, unwavering, without pause, till you are holding your breath as it begins to climb the hills away yonder.

It is gone.

The smoke blue clouds hang lower and heavier, the hills stand more grimly solemn and sombre, the wind is cold, the lake darker and more sullen, and the beauty has gone out of the marsh.

Then—then it is night.

But you do not forget the *Light*.

You know it still shines—somewhere.

CHAPTER II

SLIPPING AWAY INTO THE WILDERNESS

It was on the 15th of July, 1903, that Leonidas Hubbard, Jr., my husband, with two companions, set out from Northwest River Post, near the head of Lake Melville, for a canoe trip into the interior of Labrador, which be hoped would not only afford him an interesting wilderness experience but also an opportunity to explore and map one, and perhaps both, of these rivers, the Northwest River draining Lake Michikamau to Lake Melville, and the George River draining the northern slope of the plateau to Ungava Bay.

Misled by information obtained at the post, which corresponded with the indications of the map he carried, that of the Geological Survey of Canada, Mr. Hubbard took the Susan River, which enters Grand Lake at the head of a bay five miles from its western end. The Susan River led them, not by an open waterway to Lake Michikamau, but up to the edge of the plateau, where they became lost in the maze of its lakes. When within sight of the great lake the party was forced to begin a retreat, which Mr. Hubbard did not survive to complete. He died in the far interior, and the object of his expedition was not achieved.

It seemed to me fit that my husband's name should reap the fruits of service which had cost him so much, and in the summer of 1905 I myself undertook the conduct of the second Hubbard Expedition, and, with the advantage of the information and experience obtained by the first, a larger crew and a three weeks' earlier start, successfully completed the work undertaken two years before.

My decision to undertake the completion of my husband's work was taken one day in January of 1905. That evening I began making my plans and preparations for the journey. Towards the end of May they were completed, and on the evening of the 16th of June I sailed from Halifax for Labrador, arriving at Northwest River Post, the real starting-point of my journey, on Sunday morning, June 25th.

It was with characteristic courtesy and hospitality that M. Duclos, who was in charge of the French trading post, placed himself and his house at my service, and our coming was celebrated by a dinner of wild goose, plum pudding, and coffee. After the voyage from Halifax it seemed good to rest a little with the firm earth under foot, and where the walls of one's habitation were still. Through the open windows came the fragrance of the spruce woods, and from the little piazza in front of the house you could look down and across Lake Melville, and away to the blue mountains beyond, where the snow was still lying in white masses.

The settlement at Northwest River consists mainly of the two trading posts, the French post with its three buildings—the house, store and oil house—on the right bank of the river, close to its discharge into Lake Melville, and higher up on the opposite shore the line of low, white buildings of the Hudson's Bay Company post. A few tiny planters' homes complete the sum total of its greatness.

Monday morning the work of preparation for departure into the wilderness began. My crew numbered four, chief among whom was George Elson, who had loyally served Mr. Hubbard in 1903, and who, with rare skill and rarer devotion, had recovered Mr. Hubbard's body and his photographic material from the interior in the depths of the following winter. The other two men were Joseph Iserhoff, a Russian half-breed, and Job Chapies, a pure blood Cree Indian. These three men were expert hunters and canoemen, having been born and brought up in the James Bay country, and they came to me from Missanabie, some 700 miles west of Montreal. The fourth was Gilbert Blake, a half-breed Eskimo boy trapper, one of the two young lads of the rescue party George Elson had sent back two years before, when his heroic, but unsuccessful, efforts to save Mr. Hubbard's life had brought him to Donald Blake's house. Through the courtesy of M. Duclos, in whose service he was employed at the time of my arrival, he was released that he might go with me. The men were splendid, capable-looking fellows, with an air of quiet dignity and self-possession about them, which comes from conscious ability and character. Gilbert was a bright-faced, merry-hearted boy, with a reputation for being a willing worker, which he fully lived up to on the journey. All seemed thoroughly to enjoy the prospect of the trip, and their assurance greatly added to my ease of mind.

A deeper touch of anxiety was added for me by information obtained at Rigolette to the effect that the Hudson's Bay Company's steamer, *Pelican*, my only means of return to civilisation before the closing in of winter, would be at the post at Ungava, my destination, the last week in August. That left us two months to make the journey, which, at the shortest, would carry us across 550 miles of Labrador wilderness. It seemed a great deal to expect, but the men were confident and only eager to be started.

The task of unpacking, rearranging, and completing my outfit was not accomplished when night came. A number of the things I had counted on procuring at the posts were not to be had—the stores being almost empty of supplies. However, M. Duclos and Mr. Cotter of the Hudson's Bay Company cheerfully raided their own domiciles to supply my lack; substitutes were improvised, and shortly after noon on Tuesday the outfit was completed and loaded into the canoes. To my great satisfaction they were found to carry the load easily, riding well out of the water.

There were two canoes, canvas covered and 19 feet long, 13 inches deep, 34 inches wide, and with each of them three paddles and a sponge. The remainder of the outfit consisted of 2 balloon-silk tents, 1 stove, 7 waterproof canvas bags, one dozen 10 lbs. waterproof balloon-silk bags, 3 tarpaulins, 392 lbs. of flour, 4 lbs. baking powder, 15 lbs. rice, 20 cans standard emergency rations, 12 lbs. tea, 12 lbs. chocolate, 60 lbs. sugar, 20 lbs. erbswurst, 1 oz. crystalose, 4 cans condensed milk, 4 cans condensed soup, 5 lbs. hard tack, 200 lbs. bacon, 14 lbs. salt. There were kitchen utensils—3 small axes, 1 crooked knife, and 2 nets. The outfit of firearms consisted of two rifles, a 45-70 with 60 rounds of ammunition, and a 38-55 with 100

17

rounds. Each of the men had a 22 cal. 10-inch barrel, single-shot pistol for partridges and other small game. Each also carried a hunting knife, a pair of light wool camp blankets, and an extra pair of "shoe-packs."

For myself, I had a revolver, a hunting knife, and some fishing tackle; one three and a quarter by four and a quarter folding pocket kodak, one panorama kodak, a sextant and artificial horizon, a barometer, a thermometer. I wore a short skirt over knickerbockers, a short sweater, and a belt to which were attached my cartridge pouch, revolver, and hunting knife. My hat was a rather narrow brimmed soft felt. I had one pair of heavy leather moccasins reaching almost to my knees, one pair of high seal-skin boots, one pair low ones, which M. Duclos had given me, and three pairs of duffel. Of underwear I had four suits and five pairs of stockings, all wool. I took also a rubber automobile shirt, a long, Swedish dog-skin coat, one pair leather gloves, one pair woollen gloves, and a blouse—for Sundays. For my tent I had an air mattress, crib size, one pair light grey camp blankets, one light wool comfortable, weighing 3 1/2 lbs., one little feather pillow, and a hotwater bottle.

It was 3.15 P.M., July 27th, when the last details of preparation were completed, and we were ready to start, with all Northwest River to see us off.

"You will be all right, Mrs. Hubbard," said Mr. Cotter. "At first I did not think you could do it, but I have changed my mind. You can do it, and without any trouble too. Good-bye, and the best of success to you."

The farewell wishes of M. Duclos and M. Fournier, his assistant, were not less enthusiastic. M. Duclos ran forward a little, kodak in hand, and as the canoe glided past up the river, he said: "I have ze las' picture, Madame."

A few minutes' paddling carried the canoes round the point, and the two posts were lost to sight.

It did not seem strange or unnatural to be setting out as I was on such an errand. Rather there came a sense of unspeakable relief in thus slipping away into the wilderness, with the privilege of attempting the completion of the work my husband had undertaken to do. Everything looked hopeful for my plans, and I was only glad to be really started on my way at last. Behind me in my canoe sat the trusty hero whose courage and honour and fidelity made my venture possible, and who took from my shoulders so much of the responsibility. Through George Elson I engaged and paid the other men of my party, and on him I relied to communicate to them my plans and my directions and desires.

It was a perfect day. The air was clear as crystal, and the water, the greenwoods, the hills and mountains with lines and patches of white upon them, the sky with its big, soft clouds made such a combination of green and blue and silver as I had never seen except in Labrador. Before five o'clock we had passed the rapid at the head of the three-mile stretch of river draining Grand Lake to Lake Melville, to which alone the natives give the name Northwest River, and turned into Grand Lake.

The thought of Grand Lake had troubled me a little. It is forty miles long and four miles wide, and only a little wind is needed to make such a body of water impassable for loaded canoes. M. Duclos had offered his yacht to take us to the mouth of the Nascaupee River, but when we were ready to start there was not enough wind to carry her past the rapid, and we decided not to wait. On entering the lake we turned to the right and landed to put up our first sails. Soon they were caught by the light breeze and, together with the quick paddle strokes, carried the canoes at a rapid pace towards Cape Corbeau, which rose high and commanding twelve miles away.

At 6 P.M. we landed for supper, hard tack and bacon and tea, and then as quickly as might be were on our way again. There was need to make the most of such perfect conditions for passing Grand Lake. Sunset, and we were nearing Cape Corbeau. Then came twilight which was almost more beautiful, and I sat sometimes thinking my own thoughts, sometimes listening to George and Job as they chatted with each other in Indian. Ten o'clock came, and still the dip, dip, of the paddles went on. Now and again they were laid across the canoe, and the pipes came out, or the tired arms rested a little. It was not till eleven that we finally turned in to camp at Silver Pine Lodge, having made twenty-two miles of our journey. The sky was still light in the north-west.

The men soon had a roaring camp fire, for it had grown cold after sunset. We had a second supper, and at 12.45 A.M. I made the last entry in my diary and went to my tent. Meanwhile, the light slowly shifted from west to east along the northern sky, but did not fade away. The men did not put up their tent, but lay beside the fire, for we meant to be up betimes and try to make the mouth of the Nascaupee River before the lake, which was already roughening a little, became impassable.

At 3 A.M. George called, "All aboard." A quick breakfast, and we were started. Paddling straight towards Berry Head we passed it about six o'clock, and by 8 A.M. were safe on the Nascaupee River, where the winds could not greatly trouble us.

The sand-hills stand about the wide-mouthed bay into which the river flows, and many little wooded islands lie at its head, and in the river's mouth, which is entirely obscured by them, so that it is not until you are close upon them that the river can be seen. For a mile we threaded our way among these islands and found ourselves at the mouth of the Crooked River where it enters the Nascaupee on the north. The two river courses lie near together for some distance, separated only by a sandy plateau, in places little more than a mile wide.

At 10 A.M. we halted for lunch, and after the meal the men lay down in the willows to sleep. I tried to sleep too, but could not. The Susan River had been so rough and hard to travel, and this river was so big, and deep, and fine. The thought of what missing it two years before had cost would not be shut out.

After a bite, at 3 P.M. we were off again, and had gone only a little way when George exclaimed, "Who's that? Why, it's a bear."

On the farther side of the river walking along the hill was a huge black bear. I had never before seen one anywhere but in the Zoo, and the sight of this big fellow enjoying the freedom of his native country gave me quite a new sensation. At first we decided not to molest him. A full supply of provisions made it unnecessary to secure game now, and at this time of the year the skin would be of no value. The men sent a few rifle shots in his direction, though not with any thought of their hitting him. They had the effect of making him quicken his pace, however, and the trail took him up to the top of the hill where, as he went leisurely along, his big form clearly outlined against the sky, he proved too great a temptation. Suddenly the canoe shot out across the river, and on the other shore ran into the mouth of a little stream at the foot of a big sand-hill.

Job hurried off with the rifle, and George and I followed as I was able. We had to cross a broad belt of tangled willows, and to know what that means, one must do it; but the prospect of at least getting on the edge of a bear chase is great inducement when once you become a little excited, and I scrambled through. The hill was steep and thickly strewn with windfalls about which the new growth had sprung up. Its top was like the thin edge of a wedge, and the farther side dropped, a steep sand-bank, to the stream which flowed at its foot. When we were hardly more than half-way up, there was the sound of a shot and a funny, little shrill cry from Job. Bruin had been climbing the sand-bank, and was nearly at the top when Job fired. The bullet evidently struck him for, doubling up, his head between his legs, he rolled over and over to the foot of the bank. When I reached the top of the hill he was on his legs again and running down along the edge of the stream. There had been only one cartridge in the rifle, and Job rushed down the hill to the canoe for more.

Joe and Gilbert had crossed the river meantime and were landing near our canoe. The stream turned abruptly round the foot of the hill close to them, and I wondered what would happen when Bruin appeared suddenly round the bend. Evidently Bruin had the best eyes—or nose—for, on coming to the bend, he turned suddenly and started back up-stream; but again changing his mind he made up over the hill where we had first seen him. I was still panting and trembling with the exertion of my climb, but I took out my revolver and sent a few shots after him. It is hardly needful to say they did not hurt the bear. When Job and Gilbert came up with the rifles to where we were standing he was just disappearing over the top of the hill, having apparently been little injured, and so the chase was not followed up.

Our camp that night was on a high sand-bank on the north shore of the river. The place chosen looked rough and unpromising to me, for the ground was thickly strewn with windfalls. All this part of the country had been burned over many years ago, and was very desolate looking. The men, however, pronounced the place "Ma-losh-an! Ma-losh-an!" (fine! fine!) and in less than an hour the tents were pitched and made comfortable. New experiences seemed to be coming thick and fast, for we had supper of porcupine down on the rocks at the shore. I did not like it.

I used my air mattress that night, building it up at the head with my dunnage bag, and at the foot with boughs. My hot-water bottle was also called into requisition, for it

20

was cold. They were both better than I had hoped, and I slept as comfortably as if in the most luxurious apartment.

CHAPTER III

CLIMBING THE RAPIDS

The call "All aboard," came at about six o'clock on Thursday morning. We had breakfast, and started at 8 A.M. A cold northwest wind was blowing, and an occasional light shower fell. The sand-hills on either side of the river grew higher as we went up, with always the willows along the water edge. Miles ahead we could see Mounts Sawyer and Elizabeth rising blue and fine above the other hills, and thus standing up from the desolation of the burnt lands all about; they came as a foreword of what was awaiting us further on.

Not far from camp we took another porcupine. There were beaver signs too, willows cut off and floating downstream along the shore. Leaning over, Job picked one up and handed it back to me to show me how cleverly they do their work. A rabbit ran up from the water edge. Now it was a muskrat lying in among the willows. He was evidently trying to decide which way to go, and in a moment or two began swimming straight towards the pistols that were being loaded for him. I was a little startled and exclaimed "Why, what's the matter with him? Is he hurt?" Whereupon the men laughed so heartily that the rat almost escaped. I did not understand that it was the swift current which was carrying him against his will directly towards us, and could only think that he must have been sick, or hurt perhaps, to make him do so strange a thing. From that time forward, "What's the matter with him? Is he hurt?" became a byword in camp.

Thirteen miles above Grand Lake we reached the portage route by which the Indians avoid the roughest part of the river. It leads out on the north bank opposite the mouth of the Red Wine River, passing up to the higher country, through a chain of lakes, and entering the river again at Seal Lake. By this route the Indians reach Seal Lake from Northwest River in less than two weeks, taking just twenty-one days to make the journey through to Lake Michikamau.

The trappers told us that, going by the river, it would take a month to reach Seal Lake. I wished very much to keep to the river route, because Mr. Hubbard would have had to do so had he not missed the way, there being no Indians within reach, at the time he made his journey, from whom we could obtain information. Yet our time was short. From an Indian, whom we found at Northwest River, I had a map of the portage; but it was crude, and we should not be able to make the trip as quickly as the Indians even at best. It was quite possible that a good deal of time might have to be spent looking for the trail, for it was old and would not be easily found. It was hard to decide what was best to do.

Going ashore the men hastily examined the trail. The council which followed resulted in a decision to keep to the river. The work would be harder, but we should probably make as good progress and reach Seal Lake as soon as by going through the lakes.

Above this point the river swings more to the north, and the current grows swifter as you ascend. A little before noon we landed at Point Lucie, a high, sandy point, which stands out into the river at the foot of the first rapid. Here the trappers leave their boats and make no attempt to take canoes farther up, but portage their provisions and traps the remaining 40 miles to Seal Lake. It seemed quite thrilling to have arrived at the wonderful rapids I had heard so much about. It made me tremble a little to think of sometimes being on them in a canoe, for there was so much water, and the river looked so big.

Below Point Lucie a broad bed of loose rocks reached high up at its foot, and in the curve of the point were great sand and gravel-covered hummocks of ice. For some distance below us the farther and right bank of the river was lined with huge ice-banks, still 10 and 12 feet thick, which extended up almost to where the river came pouring out from the foot of Mount Sawyer, in a leaping, foaming torrent. At this point the river spread out over a bed of loose rocks about half a mile wide, which broke the water into channels, the widest, deepest, and swiftest of which flowed along the farther shore. The smaller and shallower ones curved into the bay above Point Lucie. A short distance above us several of these united, and from there the water was deep and swift and poured round Point Lucie with tremendous force. Around the curve of the bay and stranded in the river-bed were more ice-banks.

While George, Joe, and Gilbert were busy preparing lunch Job disappeared into the woods. Some time later he came back with four stout dry poles. They were about nine feet long and two and a half inches in diameter at the lower end. After lunch the work of shaving and shoeing them began, and the crooked knife came into use. It was fine to watch Job's quick, deft strokes as he made them ready. The "shods" George had brought from Missanabie. These were made at Moose Factory, and were the kind used throughout the James Bay country. They were hollow cone-shaped pieces of iron a quarter of an inch thick and open down one side, so that they might not break with the strain. They were 4 inches long, rounded and solid at the small end, and on either side, about an inch from the top, was a hole to admit the nail which fastened the pole in place. When finished they looked as if meant for heavy work.

All being now ready to proceed George said: "We will get in around the point, Mrs. Hubbard."

I wondered why, and concluded it must be because the water was so swift at the point. I still wondered why George did not stay to help Job; for as all their conversations were carried on in Indian, I was in darkness as to what was to happen. In silence I waited for developments. A little distance above the point, near where the water was deeper and not so swift, I looked back, and to my astonishment I saw Job poling the canoe through the swift water alone. But this was mild surprise compared with what was awaiting me.

We were soon in the canoe, and for nearly half a mile they poled up the swift current. The water was deep, and sometimes they bent over the poles till their hands dipped into the water. It seemed as if they must certainly fall overboard. I expected every minute to find myself perforce taking a header into the deep water. Sometimes we brushed the edge of a big ice-bank. The moment the poles were lifted the canoe stopped its forward movement, and if they were not quickly set again it began to slip back with the current. At last the water became too shallow and rough and we went ashore. Here the portaging began, and I climbed up over the ice-banks and walked along the shore. Even while ice and snow lingered, the flowers were beginning to bloom, and I found two tiny blue violets. On reaching the deepest part of the bay I turned to look back. Job was bringing one of the canoes up the rapid with two full portage loads in it. I could scarcely believe what I saw, and ran eagerly down to secure a photograph of this wonderful feat. But my powers of astonishment reached their limit when later I saw him calmly bringing the canoe round the bend at the foot of Mount Sawyer and up into the narrower part of the river. Now I was not alone in my wonder. Both George and Joe watched with interest equal to mine, for even they had never seen a canoeman pole in water so rough.

Job looked as if in his element. The wilder the rapid the more he seemed to enjoy it. He would stand in the stern of the canoe, right foot back, left forward with leg against the thwart, with set pole holding it steady in the rushing, roaring water while he looked the way over, choosing out his course. Then he would move the canoe forward again, twisting its nose now this way, now that, in the most marvellous fashion, and when he drove it into the rush of water pouring round a big rock the pole would bend and tremble with the weight and strain he put upon it. Sometimes I could hardly breathe while watching him. After taking one canoe some distance above the bend he went back for the second, and all the remainder of the afternoon Job climbed hills of water in the canoes.

That evening our camp was again on top of a high bank thirty feet or more above the river. Joe and Gilbert put up the tents, while down at our camp fire at the shore George made the bannocks and Job skinned, dressed, and cooked the porcupine. When it grew so dark that I could not see to write I went to help cook bannocks. It seemed good to be near the fire too, for it was growing cold. George and Job chatted merrily in Indian, Job evidently, as fond of fun as George. The fun suddenly came to an end, however, when Gilbert came down to say that the tube of my bed-pump was missing. It was too true. The thing was not to be found anywhere. It had been dropped when the stuff was handed down the bank in the morning.

It seemed a quite serious matter to me, knowing as I did from past experience that I cannot sleep on the ground long without growing very tired, when I lose my nerve and am afraid to do anything. I did not like to think of the possibility of either growing desperate and wanting to turn back or breaking down under the strain of going on. Some one would have to go back for the tube, and time was precious now. It would be trying to lose a day. While I sat rather disconsolate considering the situation, George conceived the brilliant idea of having Gilbert turn himself into an air-pump, which he did quite cheerfully, and very soon my bed was as tight and firm as need be, and peace reigned again.

When at last we assembled for supper it was nearly 10 P.M., and the stars were coming out over Mount Sawyer. The meal was a quiet one, for all were tired, and well content to listen in silence to the music of the river, as softly the night-gloom gathered unto itself the wilderness.

CHAPTER IV

DISASTER WHICH THREATENED DEFEAT

Friday morning was warm and bright. It seemed wonderful to be having so much fine weather in Labrador, and not a fly or mosquito as yet. The one nuisance we had met was mice or lemmings. They had been busy with my hat in the night, and when I came to put it on that morning I found there was a hole eaten in the crown and a meal or two taken out of the brim. There seemed to be thousands of them, and they ran squealing about everywhere, great fat fellows, some of them as big as grey squirrels. The ground was so perforated with their holes that it reminded one of a porous plaster.

While the outfit was being brought up I walked along the shore watching the rapids. The men did not like to see me go near the river at all except when in the canoe, and warned me against going to the rapids. I promised to be careful, but not to keep away altogether, for they grew more and more fascinating. I wanted to be near them and watch them all the time. They were so strong, so irresistible. They rushed on so fast, and nothing could stop them. They would find a way over or around every obstacle that might be placed before them. It made one wish that it were possible to join them and share in their strength. About a mile above camp I stepped out on a great boulder close to where they were very heavy. The rock seemed large enough so that I could scarcely fall off if I tried; but when the men came up George said: Mrs. Hubbard, you must not do that."

"Why?"

"You will get dizzy and fall in."

"But I do not get dizzy."

"Maybe you think you will not. It is all right when you are looking at the rapid, but it is when you turn that you will fall. It is very dangerous. If you are going to do that we will just turn round and go back to Northwest River."

That settled the matter.

The river here became impracticable, and Job went forward to hunt out the trail. The sandhills at this point stood back a little from the river. The low-lying land between was thickly wooded, but up on the hills the walking was good. So the trail was cut straight up the bank which was eighty feet high and very steep.

If any one supposes that cutting a trail means making a nice, smooth little path through the woods, let him revise his ideas. The hill-side was a network of new growth and windfalls. Now and again I made the mistake of calling them deadfalls. Certainly all women, and perhaps a few men, would think the mistake pardonable

26

could they see the trail which led straight over the tangled heaps of fallen tree-trunks. I watched the men carrying the canoes and their heavy loads over these with wonder almost equal to that with which I had looked at Job's work in the rapids.

The outfit made about four loads each for them, and when it was all safe on top of the hill, Joe sat down trembling like a leaf. George looked a bit shaky, and Gilbert very hot and tired.

Joe said: "In a week George and I will be hardened up so that there won't be any trembling."

Job said: "Always hard."

By noon it had grown very hot. There was scarcely a stir in the air, and the sun beat down on the sand-hills in no gentle manner. The perspiration ran down the men's faces as they carried, and the flies were beginning to come. After lunch Job set up two impromptu wigwams, stringing a tarpaulin over each, and under these shelters the men rested till 4 P.M. By camping time the outfit had been moved up over the portage about a mile, and I had learned something more about what packing means.

All day it had been slow, hot work, and the men were tired. I thought I would take a hand in making camp and getting supper. We had a beautiful camping-place, its only drawback being the distance from the water supply, for we were now 200 feet above the river, and some distance back from it. The ground was dry and moss covered, and the scattered spruce supplied the carpets for the tents which were soon ready for the night.

There were bannocks to be made again, and I helped to cook them. It was no small surprise to find how much art there is in doing it. At first I thought I could teach the men a lot of things about cooking bannocks, but it was not long before I began to suspect that I had something to learn. They were made simply with the flour, salt, baking-powder and water, but without any shortening. This made them tough, but they carried better so. As George said: "You can throw them round, or sit on them, or jump on them, and they are just as good after you have done it as before."

In cooking them a piece of the dough is taken and worked into a round lump, which is pressed flat into a frying-pan. It is then placed before the fire till the upper side of the bannock is slightly browned, when it is turned and replaced till the other side is browned. As soon as the bannock is stiff enough to stand on its edge it is taken out of the pan to make room for more, and placed before a rock near the fire, or on a pair of forked sticks until it has had time, as nearly as can be calculated, to cook halfway through. Then it is turned again and allowed to cook from the other side. In this process the possibilities in the way of burning hands and face, and of dropping the bannocks into the fire and ashes are great. I seemed to take advantage of them all, but if my efforts were not much help they certainly furnished amusement for the men. The task is a long one too, and it was nine o'clock when supper was ready.

Job, who had been absent for some time, returned now with a report that three-quarters of a mile further on we could again take the river. Despite the day's work he looked all alive with interest and energy. He loved to pole up a rapid or hunt out a trail just as an artist loves to paint.

Supper over, we sat at the camp fire for a little while. The sunset light still tinged the sky back of Mount Sawyer, and from its foot came up the roar of the rapid. Now and again a bird's evening song came down to us from the woods on the hill above, and in the tent Joe was playing softly on the mouth organ, "Annie Laurie" and "Comin' through the Rye." After I had gone to my tent the men sang, very softly, an Indian "Paddling Song."

A stream of bright sunlight on the roof of my tent roused me on Saturday morning, and mingling with the sound of the river came again that of the "Paddling Song." At breakfast all were exclaiming over the wonderful weather, George insisting that he did not believe this could be Labrador at all.

That morning I was to make my maiden attempt at following a new trail, and when the last load was ready I went first to try my fortunes. The trail meant just a little snip off the bark of a young tree here, the top of a bush freshly broken there, again a little branch cut showing that the axe had been used. There was not a sign of any path. The way was not always the easiest, and sometimes not the shortest, but it was always the quickest. My heart quite swelled with pride when I reached the river at 8.30 A.M. having missed the trail but once, and having found it again with little delay. Already it had grown hot on the hills, and the mosquitoes were beginning to come, so that it was good to be back at the river again; but before the men went away for more loads I had to promise very solemnly that I would not go on the rocks by the rapids.

By noon the whole outfit was at the river, we had lunch, and the men rested an hour and then we were off again. A mile of paddling and two short portages brought us to the head of what the trappers call "Three Mile Rapid." The river was very picturesque here, and in midstream were great swells which curled back like ocean breakers as the torrent of water poured over the boulders of the riverbed. I smile now remembering how I asked George if be thought I should see anything so fine as this rapid on, the rest of my journey.

Splendid as the rapids were, it was a great relief to reach smooth water again, though the current was still swift. Passing a bend half a mile above we came in sight of a beautiful wooded island, and saw that we had reached the edge of the burned-over country. It would scarcely be possible to convey any adequate idea of the contrast. The country had been grand with a desolate sort of grandeur softened by the sunshine and water and the beautiful skies, but now the river with its darkly-wooded hills was not only grand but was weirdly beautiful as well.

When we had passed Mabelle Island the hills seemed to close round us and were covered with tall, pointed evergreens, so dark in colour as sometimes to seem almost black. Always these have been beautiful to me, with a mysterious kind of beauty which sends through me feelings akin to those I had when as a child I dreamed over the wonderful pictures the Frost King left in the night on the window panes. The river ahead was too rough to proceed along the south shore, and the men decided to cross. It was very fearsome looking. Through a narrow opening in the hills farther up, the river came pouring from between dark, perpendicular walls of the evergreen in a white, tossing rapid, widening again to one only less turbulent. A heavy cloud hung over us, throwing a deeper shade on the hills and turning the water black save for the white foam of the rapids, while down the narrow valley came a gale of hot wind like a blast from a furnace. We turned out into the river, and all paddled as if for life. The canoe danced among the swells, but in spite of our best efforts the rapid carried us swiftly down. It was a wild ride, though we reached the other shore in safety, and looking up the river I wondered what might be in store for us beyond that narrow gateway. When we passed it would the beyond prove as much like Hades as this was suggestive of it? It seemed as if there we must find ourselves within the mysteries.

After we landed, George turned, and in mildly approving tone said: "I have seen lots of men who would jump out of the canoe if we tried to take them where you have been just now."

Job's quick eye had seen that the canoes could be taken through the narrows on the north shore. And when this part of the river was passed all suggestion of Hades vanished. There stretched before us Mountain Cat Lake, for beauty, a gem in its setting of hills. It was half a mile wide and two miles long. In the lower part were two small wooded islands, but the upper part was clear. Long spruce covered points reached out into its waters, which still flowed so swiftly that instead of paddling we poled along the shore. It was camping time when we reached the head of the lake, where the river comes down round a fine gravel point in a decided rapid.

George remarked: "That would be a fine place for Sunday camp."

"Then why not camp there?" I asked.

"Oh, no," he replied emphatically; "that would not do at all. There would be no Sunday rest for me. I'd have to be watching you all the time to keep you away from that rapid."

A little way up the river we came to another point which seemed even finer than the one at the head of the lake, and on this we made our Sunday camp. There was no noisy rapid here. On the opposite shore a long wooded hill sloped down to a point a mile above camp, round which the river came from the west. The sun was almost touching the hill-top, and below were low, gravel flats covered with fresh spring green and cut by little waterways, still as glass, and reflecting the sunset colours. In the river above us were small wooded islands, and away beyond them the blue ridges. It would have been beautiful at any time, but now in the calm evening, with the sunset light upon it, it was peculiarly so, and seemed in a special way to accord with the thought of the Sabbath rest. There was not a word spoken in reference to it, but about the men and in the way they did their work was something which made you feel how glad they were a resting time had come.

When the outfit had been landed, and the canoes drawn up on shore, George walked up the bank a little way, and there, with folded arms, stood quite still for some time looking up the river.

Presently I asked: "What are you thinking, George?"

"I was just thinking how proud I am of this river," he replied.

It seemed luxurious on Sunday morning to be able to loiter over washing and dressing, to get into clean clothes, to read a little, and to look at the day itself. I had strained both feet the day before, and they were quite swollen, but did not hurt very much. My hands and face, too, were swollen and sore from the bites of the flies and mosquitoes. Having a rooted dislike to wearing a veil, I had deferred putting one on; but it was plain now that Labrador flies were soon to overrule all objections. When breakfast was announced at 10.30 A.M. the men had been for a swim, and appeared shaved and in clean clothes—Joe and Gilbert in white moleskin trousers. Everything was done in lazy fashion. Everyone loitered. It was washing day for all, and by noon the bushes along the shore were decorated in spots in most unwonted fashion. Later, walking up the shore a little way I came upon Gilbert cutting Joe's hair.

In the afternoon the men lay in the tent or on the bank under the trees reading their Bibles and singing very softly, almost as if afraid of disturbing the stillness of "the silent places," some of the fine old church hymns. A thunderstorm passed later, but it lasted only a short time, and the evening was fine. Job took a canoe and went up the river scouting. As we sat on the shore by the camp fire, after 9 P.M., and supper just ready, he came floating down again. The river carried him swiftly past us and he called "Good-bye, Good-bye." Then all at once the canoe turned and slipped in below the point. He reported the river rapid as far as he went or could see.

Monday we started at 8.30 A.M., crossing to the other shore, where I walked along a bear trail on the flats, while the men brought the canoes up by poling and tracking. The morning was wonderfully clear, and millions of dewdrops glistened on the low growth. The "country," or "Indian," tea which grew in abundance was in blossom, and the air was filled with fragrance. It seemed to me the most beautiful morning we had yet had.

As the river grew more and more difficult part of the outfit had to be portaged. Two miles above camp about half a load was put into one of the canoes, and slipping the noose of a tracking line round the bow George and Gilbert went forward with it, while Job and Joe got into the canoe to pole. Had it not been for my confidence in them I should have been anxious here, for the river was very rough, and close to shore, where they would have to go, was a big rock round which the water poured in a way that to me looked impassable. But I only thought, "They will know how to manage that," and picking up my kodaks I climbed up the bank to avoid the willows. I had just reached the top when looking round I saw the canoe turn bottom up like a flash, and both men disappeared.

I stood unable to move. Almost immediately Joe came up. He had caught the tracking line and held to it. Then I saw Job appear. He had not been able to hold to the canoe. The current had swept him off, and was now carrying him down the river. My heart sickened at the sight, and still I could not move. Then an eddy caught him, and he went down out of sight again. Again he appeared, and this time closer to us, for the eddy had somehow thrown him in shore where the water was not so deep. He was on his back now and swimming a little, but could neither get up nor turn over. I wondered why the men stood motionless watching him. Then it dawned on me that George was holding the canoe, and I found my voice to shout: "Run, Joe." Joe's own experience had for the moment dazed him, but now he suddenly came to life. Springing forward, he waded out and caught Job's hand before he was carried into deep water again. As he felt himself safe in Joe's strong grasp, Job asked: "Where is Mrs. Hubbard? Is she all right?"

At first he did not seem able to get up, but when George, on reaching the canoe, turned it right side up, and to the utter astonishment of every one, it appeared that nearly the whole load was still in it—the sight revived Job. He got up and came ashore to the canoe, which was found still to contain the two tents, one rifle, my fishing-rod, the sextant, and artificial horizon, a box of baking-powder, a box of chocolate, my sweater, three of the men's coats, and one tarpaulin. It seemed nothing less than miraculous, for the little craft had been bottom up for several minutes. During the reckoning Job heartened rapidly, and was soon making a joke of the experience, though this did not hide the fact that he had been well shaken up.

For a time thankfulness at the escape of the men, and that so much of the outfit had been saved, made me oblivious of everything else. Then gradually it came to the minds of the men what was missing, but it was some time before the list was complete, and I knew that we had lost all the axes, all the frying-pans, all the extra pole-shods, one pole, one paddle, the crooked knife, two pack-straps, one sponge, one tarpaulin, my stove, and Job's hat and pipe. The loss of the axes and the pole-shods was the most serious result of the accident, and I wondered how much that would mean, but had not the courage to ask the question. I feared the men would think they could not go on without the axes.

Soon they began to upbraid themselves for putting both tents and all the axes into the same canoe; but there was no mention made of turning back. All seemed only thankful that no lives were lost. While Job and Joe were changing their wet clothing, George and Gilbert, as quickly as possible, prepared lunch. Job, however, was very quiet during the meal, and ate almost nothing. Later, however, I could bear George and Joe in fits of laughter. Job was entertaining them with an account of his visit to the fishes. According to his story, he had a most wonderful time down there.

CHAPTER V

TO THE BEND OF THE RRVER

Beyond this point our progress was slow and difficult. There were days when we made less than two miles, and these were the discouraging days for me, because there was ever hanging over me the thought of the necessity of reaching Ungava by the last week in August—if I meant to catch the ship there. However, by poling and tracking, by lifting and dragging the canoe through the shallow waters near the shore, or again by carrying the entire outfit over the sand-hills or across boulder-strewn valleys, we won gradually forward.

It frightened me often to see the men take their packs where they did. Sometimes it was over a great bed of boulders, where the reindeer moss was growing. This moss is a delicate grey-green colour, exquisitely beautiful in form as well, and as a background for the dark spruces is wonderfully effective. We found it growing luxuriantly almost everywhere, except in the burned districts, and in places it is six inches in height. When dry, it is brittle, and may be crumbled to powder in the hands, but when wet is very much the consistency of jelly, and just as slippery. Through the wooded land the soil appeared to be simply a tangle of fallen and decayed tree-trunks grown over with thick moss of another variety, in which you sank ankle deep, while dark perilous looking holes yawned on every side, making you feel that if once you went in you might never appear again. Sometimes our way led along a fine bear trail on a sandy terrace where the wood growth was small and scattered, and where the walking was smooth, and even as that of a city street, but much softer and pleasanter. There were many bear trails through this lower Nascaupee country, though we did not again see any bears, and one might actually think the trails had been chosen with an eye to beauty. The woods were very fine, the spruces towering far above us straight as arrows. They were, many of them, splendid specimens of their kind, and one I measured was nine feet in circumference. Here and there some balsam was found among the spruces. These were true virgin forests, but their extent was limited to the narrow river valleys. Out beyond, the hill-tops rose treeless and barren.

On the portages the outfit was taken forward by short stages, and I had a good deal of waiting to do. The men did not like to leave me alone lest I might possibly encounter a bear, and I had many warnings to keep my rifle ready, and not to leave my waiting-place. Secretly I rather hoped a bear would come along for I thought I could manage him if he did not take me unawares.

Besides the interest of watching for the bear I hoped to meet, I had, while we travelled in the more open parts, the hills both up and down the river to look at, and they were very beautiful with their ever-changing colour. Mount Sawyer and Mount Elizabeth were behind us now, and away ahead were the blue ridges of hills with one high and barren, standing out above the rest, which I named Bald Mountain. I wondered much what we should find there. What we did find was a very riotous rapid and a very beautiful Sunday camp.

32

Waiting in the lower wooded parts was not as pleasant. Once I announced my intention of setting up my fishing-rod and going down to the river to fish, while the rest of the outfit was being brought up. Sudden consternation overspread the faces of the men. In a tone of mingled alarm, disapproval, suspicion, George exclaimed: "Yes; that is just what I was afraid you would be doing. I think you had better sit right down there by the rifles. There are fresh bear tracks about here, and Job says they run down there by the river."

I could not help laughing at the alarm I had created, but obediently sat down on the pile of outfit by the rifles, strongly suspecting, however, that the bear tracks were invented, and that the real fear was on account of the river. It began to be somewhat irksome to be so well taken care of.

The mosquitoes and flies were now coming thick and fast. I thought them very bad, but George insisted that you could not even call this a beginning. I wore a veil of black silk net, but the mesh was hardly fine enough, and the flies managed to crawl through. They would get their heads in and then kick and struggle and twist till they were all through, when they immediately proceeded to work. The men did not seem to care to put their veils on even when not at work, and I wondered how they could take the little torments so calmly.

On the morning of July 6th we reached the Seal Islands expansion. Around these islands the river flows with such force and swiftness that the water can be seen to pile up in ridges in the channel. Here we found Donald Blake's tilt. Donald is Gilbert's brother, and in winter they trap together up the Nascaupee valley as far as Seal Lake, which lies 100 miles from Northwest River post. Often in imagination I had pictured these little havens so far in the wilderness and lonely, and now I had come to a real one. It was a tiny log building set near the edge of the river bank among the spruce trees. Around it lay a thick bed of chips, and scattered about were the skeletons of martens of last winter's catch. One had to stoop a good deal to get in at the narrow doorway. It was dark, and not now an attractive-looking place, yet as thought flew back to the white wilderness of a few months before, the trapper and his long, solitary journeys in the relentless cold, with at last the wolfish night closing round him, it made all different, and one realised a little how welcome must have seemed the thought and the sight of the tiny shelter.

In the tilt there was no window and no floor. All the light came in through the doorway and a small hole in the roof, meant to admit the stove pipe. Hanging on the cross beams were several covered pails containing rice, beans, flour, lard, and near them a little cotton bag with a few candles in it. Thrown across a beam was a piece of deerskin dressed for making or mending snow-shoes; and on a nail at the farther end was a little seal-skin pouch in which were found needle, thread, and a few buttons. A bunk was built into the side of the room a few feet above the ground, and lying in it an old tent. Beside a medley heap of other things piled there, we found a little Testament and a book of Gospel Songs. The latter the men seemed greatly pleased to find, and carried it away with them. We took the candles also, and filled one pail with lard, leaving one of the pieces of bacon in its place. Already we were regretting that we had no lard or candles with us. They had been cut out of the list when we feared the canoes would not hold all the outfit, and later I had forgotten to add them. The men were hungry for fried cakes, and the lard meant a few of these as a treat now and then.

Gilbert had hoped to find an axe here, but although be hunted everywhere there was none to be found. He did, however, get his little frying-pan and a small pail which made a welcome addition to our depleted outfit.

That day we portaged nearly all the afternoon. It was rough, hard walking, and occasional showers fell which made it worse. There was many a wistful glance cast across to the other shore where we could see a fine sand terrace. There the walking must be smooth and easy; but we could not cross, the rapids were too heavy.

During the afternoon we found the first and only fresh caribou tracks seen in the lower Nascaupee valley. A pair of fish eagles, circling high above us, screamed their disapproval of our presence there. We saw their nest at the very top of a dead spruce stub, some sixty feet or more above the ground. This was one of the very many things on the trip which made me wish I were a man. I could have had a closer look at the nest; I think I could have taken a photograph of it too. Now and then came the sweet, plaintive song of the white-throated sparrow.

Towards evening it began to rain fast, and as if with the intention of keeping at it; so George called a halt. As I sat down on a pile of outfit he opened up the men's tent, and, spreading it over me, directed me to wait there till my own was ready. George's tone of authority was sometimes amusing. Sometimes I did as I was told, and then again I did not. This time I did, and with my rifle on one side and my fishing-rod on the other, to hold the tent up, I sat and watched them making camp and building the fire.

All day the mosquitoes and flies had been bad, but now the rain had coaxed them out in redoubled force, and they were dreadful. I could feel how swollen my neck and ears were, and wondered how I looked; but I was rather glad that I had no mirror with me, and so could not see. Now and then I had spoken of my suspicions as to what a remarkable spectacle I must present. George, manlike, always insisted that I looked "just right"; but that night, in an unguarded moment, he agreed with me that it was a good thing I had not brought a mirror. For the first time we went into a wet camp.

It poured steadily all day Friday, and we did not attempt to go forward. I slept again after breakfast, and then did some mending, made veils, and studied a little. It was very cold and dismal; but the cold was always welcome, for it kept the flies and mosquitoes quiet. Our camp was on high ground, and from the open front of my tent I could look down over a steep bank thirty feet to the river, racing past with its ceaseless roar. Sometimes I wished I could reach out and stop it just for a minute, and then let it go again. I wished rainy days might not come often, though I fully expected that they would. About 3 P.M. I heard a stir outside and going out found

George and Gilbert making a fire. It was not so simple a matter now without an axe. The small stuff had to be broken, and then whole trees were dragged bodily to the spot and laid on to be burned off a piece at a time. When fallen stuff was scarce, standing dead trees were by hard labour pushed over and brought in. The big fire felt very good that day.

It was not raining quite so fast now, and after dinner I sat watching George while he mended my moccasin where the mice had eaten it, and sewed the moleskin cartridge pouch to my leather belt. He finished putting the pouch on, and handed the belt back to me with a satisfied smile. Instead of taking it I only laughed at him, when he discovered he had put the pistol-holster and knife-sheath on wrong side first. There was no help for it; it had to come off again, for the sheaths would not slip over either buckle or pouch. I comforted him with the assurance that it was good he should have something to do to keep him out of mischief. When the mistake had been remedied he showed me how to make a rabbit-snare. Then the rain drove me to my tent again, and I had supper there while the men made bannocks. It was horrid to eat in the tent alone.

The barometer was now rising steadily, and I went to sleep with high hopes of better weather in the morning. When I awoke the sun was shining on the hills across the river. How welcome the sight was! Everything was still wet though, and we did not break camp till after dinner. I did some washing and a little mending. The mice had eaten a hole in a small waterproof bag in which I carried my dishes, dish-towel, and bannock, and I mended it with some tent stuff. An electrician's tape scheme, which I had invented for mending a big rent in my rubber shirt, did not work, and so I mended that too with tent stuff. How I did hate these times of inactivity.

It was one o'clock when we started forward again, and all afternoon the portaging was exceedingly rough, making it slow, hard work getting the big pile of stuff forward. To add to the difficulties, a very boisterous little river had to be bridged, and when evening came we had gone forward only a short distance. We had come to a rather open space, and here the men proposed making camp. Great smooth-worn boulders lay strewn about as if flung at random from some giant hand. A dry, black, leaflike substance patched their surfaces, and this George told me is the *wakwanapsk* which the Indians in their extremity of hunger use for broth. Though black and leaflike when mature, it is, in its beginning, like a disk of tiny round green spots, and from this it gets its name. *Wakwuk— fish-roe;* wanapisk_—a rock.

It was a very rough place, very desolate looking, and far from the river. It made me shudder to think of spending Sunday there. So the men were persuaded to try to reach the head of the rapid, which was three-quarters of a mile farther on, taking forward only the camp stuff. We were now travelling along the foot of Bald Mountain seen from the hill on Monday, and passing what is known by the trappers as North Pole Rapid, which was the wildest of the rapids so far. The travelling was still rough, and the men were in a hurry. I could not keep up at all. George wanted to carry my rifle for me, but I would not let him. I was not pleased with him just then.

We reached the head of the rapid, and it was beautiful there. A long terrace stretched away for miles ahead. It was thinly wooded, as they all were, with spruce and a few poplars, smooth, dry, and mossy, and thirty feet below us was the river with North Pole Brook coming in on the other side. It was an ideal place for Sunday camp.

Though it rained hard through the night the morning was beautiful, and again I breathed a little sigh of thankfulness that we were not in the other desolate place farther back. The day would have been a very restful one had it not been for the flies which steadily increased in numbers, coaxed back to life and activity by the warm sunshine. I wanted very much to climb the mountain behind our camp in the afternoon, but I could not go alone, and the men were taking a much needed rest. So I wandered about watching the hills and the river for a while, took a few photographs, and lay in the tent. Towards evening the flies swarmed over its fly front, getting in in numbers one could not tell where or how. Still they were nothing inside to what they were outside. At supper I hated to put up my veil. They were so thick I could hardly eat. Finally George came to the rescue, and waving a bag round my head kept them off till I finished my meal.

While we were at supper Job walked silently into camp with a rifle under his arm. He had a way of quietly disappearing. You did not know anything about it till you found he was not there. Then suddenly be would appear again, his eyes shining. He had wonderfuly fine eyes, so bright that they startled me sometimes. Full of energy, quick, clever, he went straight to the point in his work always without the slightest hesitation. When you saw these men in the bush you needed no further explanation of their air of quiet self-confidence.

Job had been up as far as the bend of the river where we were to leave the Nascaupee for the trappers' cross country route to Seal Lake. A little above this bend the Nascaupee becomes impassable. It was three miles away, but Job reported, "Fine portage all the way to brook."

It was just four next morning when I heard voices at the other tent. Then all was quiet again. At six the men went past with loads. They had brought up the outfit that was left behind on Saturday. The day was fine, and we made good progress. George said: "Oh, it's just fun with this kind of portaging." It was nevertheless hot, hard work. I felt resentful when I looked at the river. It was smooth, and appeared altogether innocent of any extraordinary behaviour; yet for the whole three miles above North Pole Rapid it flowed without a bend so swift and deep that nothing could be done on it in the canoes.

All day the flies were fearful. For the first time George admitted that so far as flies were concerned it began to seem like Labrador. We ate lunch with smudges burning on every side, and the fire in the middle. I was willing that day almost to choke with smoke to escape flies; but there was no escape. In spite of the smudges there were twenty dead flies on my plate when I had finished lunch, to say nothing of those lying dead on my dress of the large number I had killed. I had to stop caring about seeing them in the food; I took out what could be seen, but did not let my mind dwell on the probability of there being some I did not see. When drinking, even while the cup was held to my lips, they flew into it as if determined to die. Their energy was unbounded, and compelled admiration even while they tortured me. How the men endured them without veils and without *words* I could not understand.

For more than two miles above our camp we kept to a fine bear trail. The walking could not have been better, and was in sharp contrast with what the trail had led us over for the last few days. Then we turned to the right and climbed to another plain above, beyond which rose the mountain.

A bear trail led along the edge of the terrace, and while the men carried I waited hopefully, rifle in hand. Ever since our bear chase back near Grand Lake my imagination turned every black spot I saw on the hills into a bear, to the great amusement of the men. But no bear appeared.

Soon mist gathered on the hills, and the specks on the plain below began to move faster and grow larger. Job led the way with a canoe. He stopped to rest at the foot of the bank, while George came past and up to the top at great speed.

"The showers are coming. We shall have to hurry or you will get wet," he said.

Every day my admiration and respect for the men grew. They were gentle and considerate, not only of me, but of each other as well. They had jolly good times together, and withal were most efficient. Gilbert was proving a great worker, and enjoyed himself much with the men. He was just a merry, happy-hearted boy. Joe was quiet and thoughtful, with a low, rather musical voice, and a pretty, soft Scotch accent for all his Russian name. He spoke English quite easily and well. Job did not say much in English. He was very reserved where I was concerned. I wanted to ask him a thousand questions, but I did not dare. George was always the gentle, fun-loving, sunny-tempered man my husband had admired.

Our camp was perhaps 100 feet above the river which here came down from the northeast round the foot of Bald Mountain, and less than half a mile below us bent away to the southeast. At the bend a tributary stream came in from the northwest to merge itself in the stronger tide, and together they flowed straight on at the foot of a long, dark-wooded ridge. Here at this stream our portage route led out from the river.

When the showers had passed we had supper, and as we sat at our meal the sun came out again, throwing a golden glow over all. Clouds lay like delicate veils along the hill-sides, sometimes dipping almost to their feet. Walking back along the edge of the terrace I watched till they gathered thick again and darkness came down over all. It was very wild and beautiful, but as an exquisite, loved form from which the spirit has fled. The sense of life, of mystery, and magic seemed gone, and I wondered if the time could come when beauty would cease to be pain.

When I returned to camp the men had gone to their tent. A tiny fire was still burning, and I sat watching it till the rain came and drove me to my little shelter again.

CHAPTER VI

CROSS COUNTRY TO SEAL LAKE WATERS

It was still raining Tuesday morning, and camp was not moved till afternoon, when we crossed the river. Though smooth here, it flowed with fearful rapidity, and in midstream carried the canoe, as if it had been a feather, at locomotive speed. Three-quarters of a mile above where we crossed the course of the river bent away to the east, and we could see the water leaping and tossing in a wild rapid as it came round through the opening in the hills. I had a great wish to see the fifteen miles of it which flows between this point and Seal Lake. I would have given much not to have to leave the river at all, but above that point it could not be travelled in the canoes, and I dared not take the time to portage which indeed would also have been impossible.

The region we were now to traverse, I learned from Gilbert, was great marten country, and so I named the tributary stream we followed, Wapustan [Marten] River. Our way led along a continuation of the river terrace we had travelled since leaving the head of North Pole Rapid. During the earliest part of that day's march it was particularly hard work to get over the windfalls. At first it seemed as if I could not; but after a struggle they were passed, and we had again a bear trail to follow. On the way we passed great beds of blossoming cloudberries, which with blossoms of the bunchberry, the Labrador tea, and the pale laurel, made up the list of flowers found so far. Towards evening we stopped to make camp at the edge of rougher country, a mile and a quarter up the Wapustan. The map grew slowly during these days, and the desire to reach Seal Lake grew stronger and stronger.

Near the camp was a big boulder, and lying round and over it were numbers of wigwam poles. They were very old, and looked as if it might have been many years since they had been used. George said it was a winter camp. In the winter time the Indians, in making their camps, dig down into the snow to a rock to build their fire. At a number of places on our journey we found poles lying round a boulder in this way.

When camp was nearly made, Job came in triumphantly waving an axe over his head. He and Joe had taken some of the outfit forward as far as Duncan M'Lean's tilt, and there had found an axe. There was great rejoicing over it. Job said he should carry the axe with the sugar after this.

I had been shooting at an owl that afternoon—from a distance that made it quite safe for the owl; and while the men prepared supper I cleaned my revolver. I was greasing it and putting some of the grease into the barrel when George said: "Don't put too much grease in it. If you put too much in the bullet will just slip and—"

"Might kill something," I finished for him.

Then came George's rare laugh. It is like a baby's in that it expresses such complete abandon of amusement.

Presently he asked: "When you were shooting at that bear the other day, where did you aim?"

"Oh, any place," I replied; "just at the bear." Peals of uncontrolled laughter greeted this announcement and cooking operations were, for the time being, suspended. When they were able to go on with the preparations for supper I could now and then hear them laughing quietly to themselves.

Bed seemed specially good that night, for I was very tired. How long I had been asleep I could not tell; but some time in the night I was awakened by sounds outside my tent, as of someone or something walking about. At first I thought it was one of the men; but presently decided it was not, and became very wide awake. I thought about the bear trail, but did not quite believe it was the bear either. Presently something shook the branches of the tree my tent was tied to, and they rattled fearfully on the tent close to my head. I sprang up, and as I reached for my revolver remembered that there were only two cartridges in it. Quickly filling the empty chambers I waited, ready to give battle to whatever it might be; but the sounds in my tent evidently alarmed the intruder, for there was silence outside after that. I was a good deal disturbed for a while, but growing calm again I finally went to sleep. In the morning the men said it was probably a rabbit jumping through the low branches of the spruce tree.

We made a mile and a half that day, and towards evening halted at the edge of a pretty little expansion in the river; it was the most charming camp we had yet found. There were a number of tiny islands here, some with a few trees, and some just the bare rock with fringes of fresh green marking the fissures. The water slipped over ledges into pretty pools, and from our camp to the other side there was a distinct downward slope. My tent was pitched about four feet from the water's edge above a little fall, and directly over an otter landing.

George warned me, "You will have to keep your boots on to-night. That otter might come along and get hold of your toes, and drag you into the river."

"Would an otter really harm me?" I asked.

"Perhaps it might be a bear instead of an otter," he replied, evading my question. "They are all great fellows for any kind of metal. If it's a bear he'll just get hold of that screw on your bed and take it right off. You'd better put a bullet inside, and then when he takes off the screw it will blow into his mouth. He'll think a fly flew down his throat, and cough. Then you could run." George's eyes were dancing with amusement at his own pictures. Presently he went on: "I think—oh! you keep a rifle in there though, don't you?"

40

"Yes."

"Don't you think you could handle salt a little better than a rifle?"

This was insulting; but I was laughing too heartily to be properly indignant, and he continued: "You might put a little salt on his tail. Maybe you could put that otter out of business, too, if you had enough salt."

A duck flew past, dropping into the water a little way above our camp, and George sprang for a rifle. He shot, but missed, which I assured him was only proper punishment for the slighting insinuations he had made in regard to my shooting. Job, and Joe went fishing after supper but got nothing. It was a fine evening with a glorious sunset, beautiful evening sky, and a splendid moon. George said: "Fine day and fine breeze to-morrow."

My sleep was not disturbed that night by either bear or otter, and we were up and started on our way the next morning at 7.30. A rough portage of three-quarters of a mile was completed some time before noon, and beyond this the canoes were kept in the water most of the day. At lunch Gilbert brought me a dandelion. I was greatly pleased to get it, and later I saw several of them. I found also blue and white violets, one of the blue ones a variety I had never seen before.

Towards evening the hills had melted away. We had come up to the top of those which, twenty miles back, had looked high, and now we could look back and down to those which there had also seemed high. A new thrill came with this being up among the hilltops, and I began to feel like an explorer.

The tents were pitched near a pool of smooth water, deep and darkened by shadows of the evergreens on either shore. On the farther side of the river were low, wooded hills, and opposite our camp a brook came tumbling through the wall of evergreens into the river. Just above the brook a high, dead stub, with a big blaze on it, showed where we were to leave the Wapustan to cross to Seal Lake.

It was not until noon on Saturday, July 15th, that we left our pretty camp, for it rained steadily in the meantime. Then we started on our cross-country trip, working up to the north, from which direction the brook flows. A two-mile carry brought us out on Saturday evening to a lake at its head. After dinner on Sunday we again went forward with a whole mile of paddling to cheer us on our way. From the head of the lake another mile of good portaging brought us at last to waters flowing to Seal Lake, and we were again in the canoes to taste for a little the pleasures of going with the tide. For long we had been going against it—and such a tide!

Our way now led through three exquisitely beautiful little lakes, to where their waters drop down over rocky ledges in a noisy stream, on their way to the lake we were trying to reach. Here on the left of the outlet we made our camp. On either side rose a high hill only recently burned over—last summer Gilbert said. George,

Gilbert and I climbed the hill back of our camp in hopes of catching a first glimpse of Seal Lake, but we could not see it. What we did see was very fine, and I stood watching it for some time after the others had gone back to camp. Eastward the great hills rose rugged and irregular, and farther away in the blue distance the range lying beyond Seal Lake, all touched to beauty by the evening light.

Slipping down the hill again, I reached camp just as the supper was ready, and after our meal George, Job, Gilbert, and I crossed to climb the hill on the other side, which rose 540 feet above our camp. It was 7.45 A.M. when we started; but a brisk climb brought us to the top in time to see the sunset, and one of the most magnificent views I had ever beheld. Some miles to the east was the lake winding like a broad river between its hills. In every direction there were hills, and lying among them little lakes that were fairy-like in their beauty. George pointed out the ridge of mountains away to the southwest which he had crossed with Mr. Hubbard, and where he thought they had crossed it from the head of Beaver Brook, their "Big River," and I named them Lion Heart Mountains.

The wind below cold on the mountain, and a shower passed over from the northeast; but it was soon gone, and the sun set over the hills in a blaze of red and gold. The way down seemed long, but when we reached camp at 10.15 P.M. it was still quite light. Joe had been fishing, and had four brook trout for my breakfast. Job and Gilbert had gone down the valley prospecting, and soon came in with the information that a mile below camp we could put our canoes into the water. Beyond, there would be two short portages, and then we should not again have to take them out of the water before reaching Seal Lake.

After I went to my tent there floated out into the quiet night the sound of the men's favourite hymns, "Lead Kindly Light," "There is a Green Hill Far Away," "Abide With Me," and, as always, the singing ended with their Indian "Paddling Song." When I put out my light at 11 P.M., a full moon was throwing shadows of the spruce boughs on my tent.

The view from the mountain-top seemed an inspiration to the party, and on Monday morning, shortly after four, I heard Job's axe making ready for the early breakfast. By 5.30 A.M. they were off with their first packs. Then all was quiet again. The tiny mirror-like lake was yet in shadow though sunlight touched the tops of its encircling hills, and I wished that I might wait, till it was time for me to go, on the summit of the one we had climbed last night. When the last load was ready I, too, went forward.

It was a glorious morning, with just such sunshine one would wish for a day so eventful. The trail led down into a valley opening eastward to Seal Lake, and walled in on three sides by the hills. On either hand reaching up their steep slopes were the spruce woods with beautiful white birches relieving their sombreness, and above--the sheer cliffs. A network of little waterways gave back images of delicate tamaracks [Larches] growing on long points between. Not a leaf stirred, and silence, which is music, reigned there. The valley was flooded with golden light, seeming to hold all

42

in a mysterious stillness, the only motion the rapids; the only sound their singing, with now and again the clear call of a bird.

After reaching the point where the canoes could again be launched, it was but a few minutes till we were in the rapids. They seem very innocent to me now, but then running rapids was a new experience, and it was tremendously exciting as the canoes sped down the current, the men shouting to each other as we went.

Two more short portages, which led down over a fine bear trail cut deep into the white moss; two brisk little runs in the canoes, and we reached smooth water, where, rounding the last bend in the brook, we could look straight away eastward into Seal Lake. A little way below the bend our brook joined a river, coming down from the northwest, which the trappers call Thomas River.

The lake was little more than a mile wide where we entered it, and extended southward nearly two miles. Gilbert pointed out the opening in the hills to the southwest where the Nascaupee River leaves the lake, and I had George and Job paddle across that I might see it. A continuation of the hills, south of the valley we had passed in the morning, swung round the south shore of the lake and culminated in what I called Santa Claus Mountain; for the outline of its rugged top looked as if the tired old fellow had there lain down to rest, that he might be ready to start out again on his long winter journey. I knew then that the beautiful valley, through which we had just passed, must be that vale where his fairies dance when it is moonlight.

About the outlet the country was wild and rugged, and from the point where the river leaves the lake the water breaks into a tossing foaming rapid. According to the trappers, the river from this point to Bald Mountain rushes down a continuous rocky slope, the hills in many places rising perpendicular from its edge.

Turning again we passed northward up the lake. It proved to be a succession of lake expansions, narrowing in one part, where it is bordered by the cliffs, and the current is very rapid. The lake is surrounded by hills of solid rock, some of those on the west arising abrupt and separate, one, Mount Pisa, distinctly leaning towards the east. Much of the surrounding country has been burned over, being now grown up with white birch and poplar, and at the narrows the angles in the cliffs are marked by lines of slender birch reaching from the water's edge to the summit. A short distance above, two large brooks enter from the east. Many of the long, low points which reach out into the lake are spruce covered, but away on the hills could be seen only the more delicate green of the birch and poplar. There are a number of islands lying mainly near the shore; and from its northern extremity an arm, which according to the trappers is thirty miles long, stretches away to the west. The river enters the lake round a low, sandy point, and about the inlet the country is lower and less rugged. On the way up we saw several seals. Gulls, ducks, and geese were there in numbers, and muskrats were plentiful.

It was after 7 P.M. when we went into camp, having made nineteen miles since morning, and every foot of the way we had been surrounded by scenes of exquisite beauty; for Seal Lake in the calm of a summer day, with the summer sunshine upon it, and the beautiful Labrador sky above, is altogether lovely. When the day's journey ended I had seen so much that was beautiful, and so varied in its beauty, that I felt confused and bewildered. I had, too, not only seen Seal Lake, I had seen the Nascaupee River flowing out of it; our camp was on the sand-point where the river enters it; and, best of all, there came the full realisation that *I* was first in the field, and the honour of exploring the Nascaupee and the George Rivers was to fall to me.

It was Monday, July 17th, three weeks less a day since we had left Northwest River post. According to the daily estimates about one hundred and fifteen miles of our journey had been accomplished, and now our next objective point was *Lake Michikamau*.

CHAPTER VII

OFF FOR MICHIKAMAU

It was well for me that a mind at rest, on at least one very important point, was my portion that night, else the nightlong fight with the mosquitoes had been horrible indeed. They seemed to come out of the ground. When despair of getting any sleep had taken possession of me, I turned with such calmness as I could muster to the task of killing them off. By diligent application I hoped in the end to secure a little respite. To interest myself I began to count my kill; but when it had reached one hundred and fifty, and yet they came, I gave it up. I was still busy when the morning light came to reveal hundreds of the vicious little beasts clinging to the slope of my tent.

At breakfast I learned that the men had fared little better. Usually they had the advantage of me where mosquitoes were concerned, for with four pipes going in the tent the mosquitoes had little chance; but that night pipes were of no avail, and there, too, the mosquitoes were master of the situation.

On Tuesday it rained, and we did not break camp till the following morning, when at 9 A.M. we were off for Lake Michikamau. Travelling was now much less difficult than it had been, though the river continued rapid. Our course, a few miles above Seal Lake, turned directly west, and as we entered Lake Wachesknipi high hills appeared ahead, showing deepest blue and purple under the cloudy sky. Again we made nineteen miles, taking on the way one partridge, two geese, and a muskrat, and camping in the evening at the foot of Red Rock Hill. Here we were destined to remain for two days on account of storms of wind and rain.

How I disliked the rainy days, for I was not very patient of delay. There was little one could do in camp, and lounging in a tent when you are not tired has few redeeming features.

After noon on Thursday Job set off to climb the hill. In the evening when I went out to supper the ground under the tarpaulins, which were strung up for shelter on either side of the fire, was covered with fresh cut shavings. Job had returned, and was carefully putting the finishing touches to a new axe handle. He said he had been up among the clouds, and reported two heavy rapids and a little lake a few miles ahead.

The following afternoon, albeit it was still raining, the men prepared to climb the hill again, and I wanted to go too. Job, however, assured me that it would be impossible as the hill was altogether too steep and slippery. I was much disappointed. It seemed such an ignominious sort of thing too, to be an explorer, and have one of my party tell me I could not do something he had already done, and was about to do again, just for the mere pleasure of it.

That it might not be too trying I had George go with me in the canoe up to the rapids. The first one, Seal Rapid, was almost three miles above our camp, and it came down from the west swinging to the south round a high sand-point and entering a small lake expansion. We landed at the head of a little bay south of the point, and crossed to the rapids. They were very wild and fine, but fortunately they did not extend far, and about three-quarters of a mile of portaging would put us on smooth water again. Here for the first time we found the rocks along the shore and in the river-bed of varied and beautiful colours. There were among them red and green and blue of many and exquisite shades—the greens being particularly beautiful. From near the head of the bay several small lakes extended westward, and through these we thought the Indians probably made their portages. It was quite late when we returned to camp, the journey back being a rather hard paddle against a strong head wind. The men had already returned from the hill, bringing a few partridges with them.

It was nearly midday on Saturday when we left Red Rock Camp, and the rain was still falling a little; but the prospects were for a fine evening and a dry camp, so it was decided to push on as already we had been delayed more than half the week. Soon the rain ceased, and, passing the portages round Seal and Cascade Rapids, we found ourselves on smooth water again. The sky cleared as we proceeded, and an occasional gleam of sunshine lent its charm to the scenes of quiet beauty through which we were passing. The river was soft and smooth as satin, with a slightly raised cushion-like appearance, that I had never noticed on smooth water before.

About the middle of the afternoon, as we rounded a bend of the river, we saw far ahead on the low drift shore, five large black objects close to the water's edge. There could be but one animal of such size and colour in this region, and I became quite stirred up over the prospect of an encounter with what looked like a bear picnic. I watched eagerly as we approached, rather wondering how we were going to manage five of them, when in a most inexplicable manner they dwindled suddenly, and my five bears had become as many ducks. It was the first time I had ever seen so striking an example of mirage. We secured three of the transformed bears, and on Sunday morning had stewed duck and fresh bannocks for breakfast.

Owing to the enforced rest through the week we decided to go forward on Sunday. After a late breakfast the task of loading the outfit into the canoes was not yet complete when Gilbert was heard to exclaim: "What's that? A duck? No, it's a deer."

Immediately all was excitement. Up in the, little lake above our camp a caribou was swimming across to the north shore. The movement in camp suddenly became electrical. The last of the load was thrown into the canoe. I stepped in as George cut the rope, which tied it to the willows, and we were off.

I was much excited at first, especially as the caribou was a long distance away, and I was sure he would reach land before we could come near enough to shoot him. He was almost ashore, and in my thought I saw him bounding up over the hills away out of our reach, and was glad. When George took the rifle to shoot I was not in the least afraid for the caribou, because I knew he would not be hit and he was not. But, Alas! I soon learned that it was not meant he should be. The bullet dropped, as it was intended to, in front of him, frightened him, and turned him back into the lake. My heart sickened as I realised what it meant. He was so near to safety. If he had only gone on. If he had only known.

The men were now almost lifting the canoe with every stroke of the paddles, and she threw the water from her bows like a little steamer. We were soon up with the caribou, and I pulled my hat down over my eyes while the deed was done. We were so close that George thought he would try to kill him with his pistol. When I looked up, after the first shot, the caribou was ploughing through the water just as before. After the second I could see him trembling and blood on the water—but he was still going on. Then I asked George to take his rifle and settle the matter quickly. He did, and the sound of the water as the caribou made his way through it ceased. I did not need to look again to know what had happened. He was towed ashore, skinned and dressed, but how I wished I could think of him as speeding over his native hills, rather than as he was. Yet, too, I knew it was well for us that we had secured the supply, of fresh meat, for although we had considerably more than half the original supply of provisions, we were still far from the journey's end.

It was a three-year-old stag, Job said, and when the operation of skinning and cutting up had been performed, we had about 250 lbs. of fresh meat added to our supply.

The day was now fine, though occasional light showers passed; but these rather added to the beauty all about us than otherwise. The river was proving a succession of lake expansions, for the most part not more than half a mile wide. Rugged, barren mountains rose in all directions, and I had the feeling of being up among the hill-tops, as if these were not whole hills, but only their tops. The trip was proving so beautiful and easy that my state of mind was one of continued surprise. I had none of the feeling of loneliness, which I knew every one would expect me to have. I did not feel far from home, but in reality less homeless than I had ever felt anywhere, since I knew my husband was never to come back to me. So far I had encountered none of the real stress of wilderness life, everything had gone well with us, everything was made easy for me; I had had no hardships to bear, and there was the relief of work to do, work which would for ever associate my husband's name with the country where he hoped to begin his explorations. For long months of darkness I had not dreamed that I could ever have the gladness and honour of doing this. Now it seemed that I might almost count on success.

As we continued our journey the river grew more and more mysterious, ending apparently in each little lake, and keeping us constantly guessing as to the direction in which our course would next lead us. The inlet in the numerous expansions was unfailingly concealed, so that not until we were almost upon it could it be made out. Most mysterious of all was the last lake of our day's journey, where the rush of the entering river could plainly be seen, but appeared to come pouring forth from a great hole in the side of a mountain. As the current swung round the upper end of the lake it made the last half hour's work decidedly exciting. We landed to camp for the night on the first portage since passing Cascade Rapid, nearly twenty miles back.

We had caribou roast for supper, and, to my surprise, I found it one of the most delicious things I had ever eaten, altogether different from any venison I had before tasted. An astonishing amount of that roast was stowed away before the camp was quiet for the night.

The northern lights were that evening very brilliant. When I put out my light at bed-time it was as if a bright moon was shining. I looked out, and above were three broad circles of light with long-pointed fingers raying up to the centre directly over my tent as I watched. It seemed like a benediction from the hand of God Himself. Gradually they drew off to the northwest in great, beautiful scrolls.

The day following, Monday, July 24th, the river continued most bewildering. Beside the portage at our camp, we had one, about half a mile long, farther up where the old trail was quite well marked, and carried us past a fall of about seven feet with a heavy rapid below. All day our way led among high hills till towards evening, when they spread out to the north and south, and we saw ahead a terraced sand plain, several miles wide, with the hills again beyond. Here, coming in from the northwest, was a brook, where, according to our map, the Indian route again leaves the river. This meant another long stretch of rough water, but our plan was still to keep to the river as far as it was possible, finding our own portage route where necessary.

The river's course was now cut deep into the plain, the banks being from thirty to forty feet in height, and the current very swift. The plain had once been sparsely, wooded but was burned over and very desolate looking now. Huckleberries, cranberries, and Labrador tea grew in profusion, and were in blossom, while patches of reindeer moss were seen struggling into life where we made our camp.

During the last part of the day's journey the current had been increasingly swift, and some distance ahead we could hear the sound of a heavy waterfall. We reached it the following morning about two miles or more above our camp. It was a beauty, about thirty feet in height. The canoes could be taken close to the foot of the fall, and after a short carry over the high, rocky point were put in the water again not twenty feet from the brink of the fall.

As the morning was fine, I had walked from camp to the fall while the men brought up the canoes. I was striding along the terrace, not thinking at all about my surroundings, when I suddenly became conscious of a most delightful fragrance, and looking down I found myself in the midst of a tangle of the long, trailing vines of the twin flower (Linnea borealis), sweetest of all Labrador flowers, with hundreds of the slender, hair-like stems bearing their delicate pink bells. How delighted I was to find it. Other Labrador flowers were beautiful, but none so lovely as this.

Above the falls the river was very rough, and in the next half or three-quarters of a mile we made three more portages, and landed a little before noon at a high, rocky point on the south shore, to find ourselves at the edge of the hill country again. Here the river was crowded between high, rocky hills where it flowed too swift and deep for either poles or paddles. We could keep to it no farther, and so made camp, for now some scouting for a portage route would be necessary.

While at dinner that day a thundershower passed. The thunderstorms of Labrador seem very mild and gentle as compared with those we are accustomed to. Later it settled to steady rain. Job went scouting, and the others lay in the tent most of the afternoon, Joe and Gilbert not feeling very well. Trouble—change of diet with a little too much of it. Job on his return in the evening reported the river bending away to the southwest a few miles farther on, and impassable as far as he could see. There would be a long portage west and south, but the country was not very rough, and a number of small lakes would give some paddling.

The following day all the men, except Job, were ill, and camp was not moved till Thursday morning. When evening came, the outfit had been taken forward three and a half miles. The three small lakes we had passed had given about one mile of paddling, and at night our camp was made at the edge of the fourth, a tiny still water pond.

The flies were that day worse than I had ever seen them. My veil proving an insufficient protection, I made myself a mask from one of the little waterproof bags, cutting a large hole in front through which I could see and breathe, and sewing over it several thicknesses of black veiling. There were as well two holes cut at the back of the ears for ventilation-these also being covered with the veiling. Pulling it over my head I tied it tight round my neck. It was most fearful and hideous to look upon, but it kept out the flies. The men insisted that I should have to take it off when we came to the Nascaupees else they would certainly shoot me. The flies were in clouds that day, and even their tapping on the outside of my mask made me shudder. I ached as I watched the men carrying their heavy loads, for it was very, very hot, and they wore no protection whatever. How they endured so uncomplainingly I could not understand, and they rarely wore their veils. It was an unspeakable relief when the clear, cool night closed in, and for a time put an end to the torture.

CHAPTER VIII

SCARING THE GUIDES

I awoke on Friday at 2.30 A.M. The morning was clear as diamonds, and from the open front of my tent I could see the eastern sky. It glowed a deep red gold, and I lay watching it. An hour later the sun appeared over the hills touching the peak of my tent with its light, and I got up to look out. The mists had gathered on our little lake, and away in the distance hung white over the river.

Gilbert was busy getting wood and preparing the breakfast. Soon I heard him at the door of the men's tent saying, "All aboard."

"Any mosquitoes this morning, Gilbert?"

"Not a one. Too cold. By Garge, but it's cold this morning! I went down to the lake and tried to wash, but I had to l'ave off. It was too cold."

Shortly I heard them at the fire. The click of the cups told me that they were taking a little tea and bannock before starting to carry. Then all was quiet, and one load had gone forward to the next lake, nearly a half mile ahead. When all but the camp stuff had been taken forward, we had breakfast, and by 7 A.M. we were in the canoes.

Our course led us south through two little lakes, with a portage between, for something more than two miles. Here the second lake bent away to the southeast, and we landed on our right at the foot of a low moss-covered ridge. Beyond this we hoped to see the river. As we climbed, new heights appeared before us, and it proved to be about three-quarters of a mile to the top, from which the ridge dropped abruptly on the west, and at its foot was a long, narrow lake. At first I thought it was the river, but, when it became clear that it was not, my heart sank a little. Had we been wrong after all? Had the river bent away to the north instead of the south as we supposed?

Job and Gilbert outstripped us in the climb, and now we saw them disappearing across a valley on our left in the direction of a high hill farther south, and we followed them. As before, new heights kept appearing as we went up, and when the real summit came in view we could see Job and Gilbert sitting on its smooth and rounded top looking away westward. How I wondered what they had found. When we came up with them there, to the west, around the south end of the opposite ridge, we could see the river flowing dark and deep as before. Above, to the southwest, were two heavy falls, and at the head of the upper and larger one the river widened. There were several islands, and it looked as if we might be coming to the expansions near the upper part of the river. One lake beside that at the foot of the mountain would make the portage route an easy and good one.

The view from the mountain top was magnificent in all directions. To the north the hills lay east and west in low, regular ridges, well covered with green woods; and thirty miles away, on a few of the highest of them, were great patches of snow lying. East and west and south were the more irregular hills, and everywhere among them were the lakes. It was very fine; but to my great regret I had left my kodaks in the canoe.

The green woods interested Gilbert, who was looking for new trapping grounds for himself and Donald Blake. We had come more than fifty miles from Seal Lake, the limit of his present trapping grounds, and he quite seriously considered the question of extending his path up to those hills the following winter.

Turning to George, I said: "Why shouldn't I come up here after dinner with my kodaks, and take some pictures while you men are making the portage? The walking is not rough, and I couldn't possibly lose my way if I tried."

He looked quite serious about it for a moment, and then said: "Well, I guess you might."

Slipping down the south end of the hill a little way to see that there were no rough places where I should be in danger of falling going down, he returned, and with the manner of one who is making a great concession said again: "I guess you can come up here this afternoon. You could go down this way and meet us at this end of the lake. You will be able to see when we come along in the canoes."

I was delighted, and after a half hour on the hill-top we started back directly towards the canoes. It was very hot among the lower and more sheltered sand-hills, and for a long time there was no running water to be found; but when we did come upon a tiny stream crossing the way, hats were quickly turned into drinking-cups for one long, satisfying drink. The miles back to camp had always a way of drawing themselves out to twice the usual length. George insisted that it was but two miles to the canoes, but to me it seemed quite four.

Lunch over, we rested a little, and then armed with two kodaks, note-books, revolver and cartridges, bowie knife, barometer and compass, I was ready for my climb. Before starting George said: "I think you had better take your rubber shirt. It is going to rain this afternoon."

I looked at the sky. It was beautiful, with numbers of silvery clouds floating lazily over the hills. It didn't look like rain to me, and I had something of a load as it was, I said: "No, I don't think I shall. I should rather not have any more to carry. It is not going to rain."

George said no more, and we started. At the little bay reaching in at the foot of the mountain we parted, and I went on up the hill. It seemed beautiful to be going off without a guard, and to think of spending an hour or two up on the hill top, quite alone, with a glorious sky above, and the beautiful hills and lakes and streams in all directions. I should be able to get some characteristic photographs and it was a perfect day for taking them. No time was wasted on the way, and the two hours proved all I had hoped.

The canoes did not come, however, and knowing that the men must have had ample time to make the portage, I decided to go down to the lake. Certainly by the time I reached it they too would be there, for a thunder-shower was coming.

When only a little way from the summit, I looked down into the valley and there, quite near where I was to meet the men, I saw something, which looked like a huge, brown bear, lying down. I stopped and watched it for a while, hardly knowing what to do. I had been deceived often, but this was not a mere black spot. It had definite shape and colour. Though I knew but little about the habits of bears, it did not seem the thing one would expect of a bear, to be lying there on the moss and rocks at that time of day. Still I did not know.

Finally, I concluded that the quickest way to settle the question was to go and see. I had my revolver, and if it proved a real bear I would not this time aim "any place; just at the bear." I hurried on trying to keep the disturbing object in sight, but I could not. When the valley was reached it was nowhere to be seen, and I concluded I had again been deceived.

The storm had now come on, and there was still no sign of the canoes. I decided that if I must be drenched and devoured, for the flies were fearful, I might as well be doing something interesting. I set off for the ridge on the further side of the lake with something of the feeling a child has who runs away from home, for it had been constantly impressed upon me that I must never go away alone, and I recognized the justice of the demand; but I meant to be careful, and probably should not go very far. Wading across the brook, which drains the lake to the river, I climbed up the ridge and was delighted to get a fine view of the falls. I went on to the top, but still there was no sign of the canoes, and I walked northward along the ridge. It was like a great mound of rock set down on the surface of the earth, its top rounded and smooth and bare, while on either side it dropped abruptly almost to the level of the lake, ending in a precipice a mile from where I had climbed it. When I reached its northern end I could see the little bay to which the men had carried the outfit.

Imagine my astonishment when, looking across, I saw the two canoes turned upside down over the stuff to keep it dry, and the men around a fire drinking tea. I was not a little annoyed to find that they were quite so ready to leave me alone in the thunderstorm, knowing that I had nothing to protect me, till suddenly I remembered how I had been advised to take my rubber shirt—and then I thought I understood. I was to have a lesson in taking good advice when I could get it.

I laughed a little and thought: "Oh! I know something better than that. This afternoon I shall I 'go where I like and do what I please,' like the little fly, and have 'one good time.'"

Taking out my revolver I fired two shots to let them know where I was, and started back along the top of the ridge to look for a place to climb down. There was a still higher ridge between me and the river, and I knew that from it I could see more. I stopped to take a photograph of a great boulder set on top of some smaller rocks, and while doing so heard two rifle shots from the other shore. Evidently they had just discovered where I was. I fired once more in reply, and then disappeared down the other side of the mountain.

It was steep, and I laughed to think how terrified they would be if they could see me; but this afternoon as I had thrown off restraint, I chose the first place where descent was possible, and let myself down along a rather wide crevice where some earth had gathered, and a few bushes were growing. I went fast too, for I meant to go just as far as I could before I was rounded up and brought into camp. Between the two ridges was a bog, and I tried to cross it to save time; but it threatened to let me in too deep, and I had to give it up and go round. I was only a little way up on the other hill when there came the sound of two rifle shots from the lower end of the lake. Evidently the discovery of my, whereabouts had aroused very spirited movement. On I went, faster than ever. The flies were desperately thick, and I kept a piece of spruce bough going constantly over my face and neck to keep them from devouring me bodily. I could feel my ears and neck wet and sticky with blood, for some of the bites bleed a good deal. Still what did flies matter when you were *free*. That afternoon I should go just as far as I thought I could, and get back to camp by dark.

To my disappointment, when I reached the top of the ridge I still could not see the river, for it disappeared between high, rocky banks, and could only be seen by walking close to the edge. I decided to go along the ridge as far as I could, and then, slipping down to the river, to return to camp that way. About two miles out on the ridge I sat down to rest and look about a little. The rain passed, and a fine breeze put the flies to rout at this highest point.

I had been seated there but a little while when, looking back, I saw one of the men, which proved to be George, running as if for life along the top of the ridge where they had first seen me. I could just make him out against the sky. Then he disappeared, I could not tell where.

After a time I began to hear shots. The sounds were very faint, but followed each other in quick succession. I laughed, and thought I knew what was happening where they came from. The shots seemed to come from the ridge I was on; but for some time I could not see any one. Finally, I caught sight of one of the men. He was waving his arms about wildly, and I could hear very faintly the sound of shouting. Then another figure appeared, and they started running towards me.

Suddenly I became frightened. Perhaps all the excitement was not on my account after all, and I began to wonder if something dreadful had happened. Had any one been hurt, or drowned? I started quickly towards them, but as soon as they were near enough for me to see their faces plainly, I knew that I had been the sole cause of the trouble. It was George and Job. The perspiration was dripping from their faces,

53

which were pale and filled with an expression, the funniest mixture of indignant resentment, anxiety, and relief, that could possibly be imagined.

When they came up I smiled at them, but there was not any answering smile. Then George began to remonstrate with me. He stood with folded arms, and serious, reproachful face, and said: "Well, I guess you very near done it this time."

"Very near done what?" I asked.

"Why, you have just about had us crazy."

"Had you crazy! What about?"

"Why, we thought you were lost."

"Didn't you see me over there on that ridge when I fired those shots?"

"Yes, we did; and when we got up to the other end of the lake we fired two shots, and we thought you would come back then. I went up the ridge to meet you, and when I saw you were not there I was sure you went down to the rapids. Then I ran down there, and when I did not find you there I thought you either fell in that rapid, or got lost."

"But I promised not to go to that rapid."

"Yes, I know you did; but I thought when you went up there on that mountain may be you would go to that rapid any way."

"Well," I said, "when I got to the end of the lake, and saw you were not coming, and the thunderstorm was coming on, and the flies were so bad, I thought I might as well be doing something nice while the storm was wetting me, and the flies were eating me."

"Yes, that is just what we said. 'Who would ever think of your going up there in that storm?'"

I laughed again, and George went on still trying to impress on me the evil of my ways.

"Job, too, he was coming running, and he was sure you were lost. When I came to meet you, and could not see you on the ridge, and then went to the rapid and could not see you there, we began to walk faster and faster, and then to run like crazy people. Poor Job, he could hardly speak, and neither could I, and out of breath, and half crying all the time. Oh, we can never trust you to go away alone agains."

54

I said: "Very well, George, I'll make a bargain with you. If I can have some one to go with me whenever I want to climb a mountain, or do anything else that I think it is necessary to do in my work, without any fuss about it, I promise not to go away alone again."

So the compact was made.

As we walked back to camp George talked. "And you did it so quick too. Why I was watching you up on that mountain where you went this afternoon, and you were so busy and running about up there, as busy as a Labrador fly. You looked just like a little girl that was playing at building something, and I thought how you were enjoying yourself. Then the first thing I knew I heard the shots on the other side of the lake. We did not see you at first. We just looked across the lake and could see nothing, and we wondered about those shots, and who could be there. Then Joe said: 'Look there, up on the mountain.'

"Then we saw you, but we never thought it was you. Then Joe said: 'Why, it's a woman.' Then we only knew it was you. Even then we could not believe it was you. Who ever would think to see you and the little short steps that you could go away there, and so quick too. Why, we couldn't believe it. The men got on to me too. They said they never saw anything like the way you do. They said they had been on lots of trips before, and where there were women too, and they, said to me they never were on a trip before where the women didn't do what they were told."

I laughed again, which George seemed to think was very hard-hearted. He looked quite as if he could not understand such callousness, and said: "Yes; you don't care a bit. Do you?" Whereupon I laughed harder, and this time he did too, a little.

Then he went on: "Oh, I just thought I was never going to see you again. I'm never going to forget about it. I was thinking about how you would feel when you knew you were lost. It is an awful thing to be lost. If I had never been lost myself I wouldn't know what it means to be lost. And what would we do if you got lost or fell in that rapid? Just think what *could* we do? Why, I could never go back again. How could any of us go back without you? We can't ever let you go any place alone after this."

Then after a thoughtful pause. "And to see you, too, the way you look. Just as if you would never scare anybody."

When we reached camp it was growing dusk. Joe and Gilbert had just finished putting up my tent. They, too, had been out on the ridge.

Though I could not help being amused at the unexpected success of my little plan to be even with them for leaving me alone in the storm, I was really sorry. I had not meant to frighten them so much. They were all very quiet, their faces, with the exception of Gilbert's, were distinctly pale, and hands trembled visibly. The brandy bottle had but once before been out, but that night, when my bags were brought in, I handed it to George, that they might have a bracer, and be able to eat supper.

Later on I was to learn that the game had not yet been played out. Again the joke was on me.

They drank it all!

CHAPTER IX

MOUNT HUBBARD AND WINDBOUND LAKE

The day following no one was astir early. I think no one slept much. I could hear from the other tent the low hum of the men's voices far into the night. Mosquitoes kept me awake. About 2 A.M. I got up, lighted my candle, and killed all I could find, and after that I had a little peace, but did not sleep much. It was then growing light.

There was a general limpness to be observed in camp that morning, aggravated by a steady downpour of rain; but before noon it cleared, and the men took all but the camp stuff forward. We had supper late to avoid the flies, the still night gathering round us as we ate. Rising close above was the dark mass of Lookout Mountain, the lake at its foot stretching away into the gloom, reflecting dimly the tinge of sunset light in the sky above. By the camp fire, after our meal, the men sat telling each other stories till Job and Joe broke the little circle and went to their tent. Then floating out on the solemn, evening silence came the sound of hymns sung in Indian to old, familiar tunes, and last the "Paddling Song." With what an intense love the one who was "gone away" had loved it all. I could not help wondering if sometimes he wished to be with me. It seemed as if he must.

On Sunday morning it rained, but cleared before noon, and at 11.30 A.M. we were on the river. That afternoon and the day following we passed the most picturesque part of the river. There were Maid Marion Falls, where the river drops fifty feet into a narrow gorge cut out of the gneiss and schists of the Laurentian rock over which it flows; Gertrude Falls, a direct drop of sixty feet, which for dignity and beauty is unsurpassed by any feature of the Nascaupee; and Isabella Falls, a system of falls and rapids and chutes extending for more than a mile, where the water poured over ledges, flowed in a foaming, roaring torrent round little rocky islands, or rushed madly down a chute. About half-way up there was an abrupt, right angle bend in the river, and, standing at the bend looking northward, you could see through the screen of spruce on the islands, high above you and half a mile away, the beginning of the river's wild mile race, as it took the first flying leap out over a wall of rocks.

The rock colouring was a deep red brown, and in some places almost purple. The perpendicular surfaces were patched with close lying grey-green moss, and in places with a variety almost the colour of vermilion. The country was not burned over, and everywhere the beautiful reindeer moss grew luxuriantly, setting off in fine contrast the tall spruces, with occasional balsams growing among them.

A mile and a half of very rough portaging brought us at 3 P.M. to the head of the falls, and there we found ourselves on a lake at last. Perhaps few will understand how fine the long stretch of smooth water seemed to us. That day the portaging had been very rough, the way lying over a bed of great, moss-covered boulders that were terribly slippery. The perspiration dripped from the men's faces as they carried, for it was very hot. The big Labrador bulldogs (flies as large as wasps) were out in force that day, as well as the tiny sandflies. One thing we had to be thankful for, was that there were no mosquitoes. The men told me that there are never many where the bulldogs are plentiful, as these big fellows eat the mosquitoes. I did not see them doing it, but certain it is that when they were about in large numbers there were very few mosquitoes. They bit hard, and made the blood run. They were so big and such noisy creatures that their horrible buzzing sent the cold chills chasing over me whenever they made an attack. Still they were not so bad as mosquitoes.

And now we were afloat again on beautiful smooth water. The lake stretched away to the southwest six and a half miles. We camped that evening on a rocky ridge stretching out in serpent-like form from the west shore of the lake above. The ridge was not more than fifty feet wide, but it was one mile long. The rocks were grown over with moss, and the willows and a few evergreens added their touch of beauty. These long narrow points were a characteristic feature of the lakes of the upper plateau. In this and the lakes above, through which we passed the day following, there were many small, rocky islands, some of them willow covered, some wooded. The shores everywhere were wooded, but the difference in size in the trees was now quite marked. They were much smaller than on the river below. The water was clear, and we could see the lake beds strewn with huge boulders, some of them reaching to very near the surface. Here we began to see signs of the Indians again, occasional standing wigwam poles showing among the green woods.

Passing four of these lakes, we came to where the river flows in from the south down three heavy rapids. On the west side of its entrance to the lake we found the old trail. The blazing was weather worn and old, but the trail was a good one, and had been much used in the days long ago. The portage was little more than a quarter of a mile long, and we put our canoes into the water again in a tiny bay above the islands.

While the men took their loads forward I set up my fishing-rod for the first time. Every day I had felt ashamed that it had not been done before, but every day I put it off. I never cared greatly for fishing, much as I had loved to be with my husband on the lakes and streams. Mr. Hubbard could never understand it, for more than any other inanimate thing on earth he loved a fishing-rod, and to whip a trout stream was to him pure delight. As I made a few casts near the foot of the rapid, my heart grew heavier every minute. I almost hated the rod, and soon I took it down feeling that I could never touch it again.

In the bay above the falls we saw a mother duck and her flock of little ones, the first we had seen so far on our trip. In the afternoon we passed up the short reach of river into another lake, the largest we had yet seen, stretching miles away to east and west, we could not tell how far. We could see, the men thought, about ten miles to the east, and twelve to fifteen west. The lake seemed to average about four miles in width. The narrowest part was where we entered it, and on the opposite shore, three miles away, rose a high hill. It seemed as if we might even now be on Michikamau, perhaps shut from the main body of the lake only by the islands. From the hill we should be able to see we thought, and so paddled towards it.

The hill was wooded almost to the top, and above the woods was the barren moss-covered summit. The walking was very rough. It seemed to me as we climbed that I should be stifled with the heat, and the flies, and the effort, but most of all with the thoughts that were crowding my mind. Instead of being only glad that we were nearing Michikamau I had been growing more and more to dread the moment when I should first look out over its broad waters. Sometimes I felt that I could never go on to the top—but I did.

The panorama of mountain, and lake, and island was very impressive. For miles in every direction were the lakes. Countless wooded islands, large and small, dotted their surfaces, and westward, beyond the confusion of islands and water around us, lay the great shining Michikamau. Still we could see no open way to reach it. Lying along its eastern shore a low ridge stretched away northward, and east of this again the lakes. We thought this might perhaps be the Indian inland route to George River, which Mr. Low speaks of in his report on the survey of Michikamau. Far away in the north were the hills with their snow patches, which we had seen from Lookout Mountain. Turning to the east we could trace the course of the Nascaupee to where we had entered it on Sunday. We could see Lookout Mountain, and away beyond it the irregular tops of the hills we had come through from a little west of Seal Lake. In the south, great rugged hills stood out west towards Michikamau. North and south of the hill we were on were big waters. The one to the south we hoped would lead us out to Michikamau. It emptied into the lake we had just crossed in a broad shallow rapid at the foot of our hill, one and a half miles to the west.

George showed me, only a few miles from where we were standing, Mount Hubbard, from which Mr. Hubbard and he had seen Michikamau; Windbound Lake and the lakes through which they had hoped to find their way to the great lake; the dip in the hills to the east through which they had passed on their long portage. He pointed out to me a little dark line on the brow of the hill where the bushes were in which they had shot the rabbit, and on the eastern slope another dark shadow showing where they had shot the ptarmigan.

So much of life and its pain can crowd into a few minutes. The whole desperate picture stood out with dread vividness. Yet I had wished very much to see what he had shown me.

At the rapid we were but a few minutes poling up to the big water south. Then after two miles of paddling, still southward, we rounded a point and looked westward straight into Michikamau and the sun. It was 5.52 P.M.

When the exclamations of delight had subsided Gilbert asked: "Do we have rice pudding for supper to-night, Mrs. Hubbard?"

That evening we camped in an island flower-garden.

CHAPTER X

MICHIKAMAU

It was the sun that did it, or else it was a scheme on the part of George and Job to work in an extra pudding. However that may have been, we found ourselves on Wednesday morning not yet on Lake Michikamau, and we did not reach it until 5.15 P.M. that day.

We started, expecting to paddle straight away west into the great lake. As we glided out on what proved to be, after all, another lake instead of an arm of Michikamau, we saw that land, not water, stretched across the western horizon. South from our island camp the shore of the lake was a low ridge sloping to the water in three distinct terraces, moss-covered and smooth as a carefully kept lawn, with here and there a clump of stunted fir trees. Four miles to the west the ridge terminated in a low point.

As we crossed the lake Job remarked that there was some current here. On nearing the point we were startled by a sudden exclamation from him. He had caught sight of a freshly cut chip on the water. We stopped, and the chip was picked up. The two canoes drew together, when it was examined closely, and an animated discussion in Indian went on. It was all interesting to watch, and a revelation to me to see an ordinary little chip create so much excitement. How much a seeming trifle may mean to the "Children of the Bush," or for that matter to any other "children," who see the meaning of things. I could not tell of course what they were saying, but I knew that the question was: "Who, beside ourselves, is in this deep wilderness?" The conclusion reached was that the wind had brought it here in the night from our own camp.

Passing the point the canoe again stopped some distance beyond it, and another brisk conversation ensued. I learned they had discovered a current coming from the south, and we turned to meet it. Following it up, one mile south and one mile west, we came to where the river flows in from the south in a rapid. This was really funny. We had comfortably settled ourselves in the belief that the rapids had all been passed. Job and Gilbert had taken off their "shoe-packs" with the prospect of a good day's paddling, and here were the rapids again. Our course for four miles above this point was up a tortuous, rapid river. It seemed to flow from all points of the compass, and, in almost continuous rapids. They were not rough, but the currents were fearfully swift, and seemed to move in all directions. These are more difficult to understand, and hence more dangerous than many of the rougher rapids.

About 2 P.M. we came out upon a lake. It was not very large, and its upper end was crowded with islands. Four miles from the outlet the lake narrowed, and the water flowed down round the islands with tremendous swiftness. Again it widened, and a mile west from the rapids we landed to climb a hill. Everyone went, and by the time I was half-way up, the men were already at the top jumping round and waving their hats and yelling like demons, or men at a polo match. As I came towards them, Gilbert shouted: "Rice pudding for supper to-night, Mrs. Hubbard." It was not hard to guess what all the demonstration meant. We could not see all the channel from our hill-top, there were so many islands; but it could be seen part of the way and what was most important we could see where it led straight west to Michikamau.

Once more in the canoes our way still led among the islands up the swift flowing water. It was not till 5.15 P.M. that we at last reached the point where the Nascaupee River first receives the waters of the great lake. Paddling against a rather strong head wind we continued westward near a long island, landing shortly before 7 P.M. on its outer shore to make our first camp on Lake Michikamau.

It was a beautiful place, and had evidently been a favourite with the Indians. There were the remains of many old camps there. Here the flies and mosquitoes were awful. It made me shiver even to feel them creeping over my hands, not to speak of their bites. Nowhere on the whole journey had we found them so thick as they were that night. It was good to escape into the tent.

Next morning I rose early. It was cloudy but calm, and Michikamau was like a pond. How I wondered what fortune would be ours in the voyage on this big water. The canoes seemed so tiny here. I called the men at 6.30 A.M., and at nine we were ready to start. Before leaving, Job blazed two trees at the landing, and in one he placed a big flat stone on which I wrote with a piece of flint Joe brought me,

HUBBARD EXPEDITION,
ARRIVED HERE, AUGUST 2ND 1905.

Underneath it I wrote the names of all the party. Then we embarked and it was "All aboard for George River!" our next objective point.

Our way led among the islands through water which seemed to promise good fishing. We put out the trolls, and waited hopefully to see what might be the prospect for testing the namaycush (great lake trout) of Michikamau for lunch. We had not long to wait. Soon I saw Joe in the other canoe hauling in his line, and a few minutes after there was a tug at mine. I got a nice little one. I had my line out a second time for just a short while when there was a harder tug on it, and I knew I had a big one. We had no gaff, and Job said we had better go ashore to land him. We did, and I was just pulling him up the beach when he gave one mighty leap and was gone. When my line came in I found the heavy wire which held the hooks had been straightened out, and he had gone off with them in his mouth. Joe's fish was a big one, about fifteen pounds, the men thought. Job said mine was bigger.

We had lunch on an island that day. The men boiled the whole of the big fish, except a little that they fried for me. George ate the head boiled, which be says is the best part. It was all delicious. I cleaned my little one carefully, and placing some willow boughs about it, laid it in the shade until we should be starting. Then after all my care we went away and forgot it. On the island we found the whitened antlers and skull of a young caribou stag. Joe cut off one of the points, and I used it after that to wind my trolling line.

During the afternoon there was more wind, and the lake grew rougher. It was fine to see the way the men managed the canoes. Sometimes we seemed almost to lose ourselves in the trough of the big waves, but there was not a dipper of water taken in. There was a head wind and hard paddling for a time, but towards evening it grew calmer, and the lake became very beautiful. In the distance we saw several large masses of floating ice, and lying far away in the west were many islands. The sky above was almost covered with big, soft, silver clouds and as the sun sank gradually towards the horizon the lake was like a great field of light. Once we stopped to listen to the loons calling [Great Northern Divers]. They were somewhere out on the glittering water, and far apart. We could not see them, but there were four, and one wild call answering another rang out into the great silence. It was weird and beautiful beyond words; the big, shining lake with its distant blue islands; the sky with its wonderful clouds and colour; two little canoes so deep in the wilderness, and those wild, reverberant voices coming up from invisible beings away in the "long light" which lay across the water. We listened for a long time, then it ceased.

We camped early that night south of the bay on the farther side of which the hills reached out to the west, narrowing the lake to about seven miles. The bay was between four and five miles wide, and it was too late to risk crossing it that night. George said if it were still calm in the morning they would take just a bite and a cup of tea, and start. We could have breakfast on the other shore.

During the night a north wind sprang up, and though soon calm again the lake was stirred up, and all the rest of the night and the early morning we could hear the waves rolling in on the beach. From dawn the men were out, now and again, to see if it were fit to start, but it was 10 A.M. before we were on the water. On one of the islands where we landed during the morning we found the first "bake-apple" berries. They were as large as the top of my thumb, and reddened a little. Though still hard they already tasted like apples. We lunched on an island near the north shore of the bay. While at our meal the wind changed and was fair for us, so we started, hoping to make the most of it. Crossing through a shallow which separated what had looked like a long point from the hills, we came out to the narrower part of the lake. Here the hills on the east shore were seen to recede from the lake, stretching away a little east of north, while between, the country was flat and boggy. A short distance further on we landed to put up sails. A ptarmigan and her little family were running about among the bushes, and the men gave chase, coming back shortly afterwards with the mother bird and her little ones.

Towards evening we put out our trolls, and I caught one big brook trout, one little namaycush, and a big one a twenty-pounder. This time he did not get away, though I strongly suspect this may have been because Job landed him. We camped late in a swampy place, and while the men put up camp I cleaned my three fish. The big one was so big that I could hardly manage him. I had just opened him up and taken out the inside and was struggling to cut off his head when somehow my hunting-knife touched his spinal cord in a way that made his tail fly up almost into my face. I sprang up with a shriek but suddenly remembered he really must be dead after all, and returned to my task. Presently Job emerged from the bushes to see what was the trouble. He suggested that I had better let him clean the fish, but I declined. Finally I did get the head off, and soon carried my fish to the camp in triumph. The big one was boiled for supper, and, oh! how good it tasted, for all were desperately hungry. The night was clear and cold, and after supper I sat at the camp fire till quite late—- reluctant to leave it. Finally it died down, and leaving the glowing embers to burn themselves out, I went to my tent.

We were off early next morning with a fine southwest wind, and were at the head of the lake sooner than we had expected. From here we had to cross almost to the west shore to reach the bay at the north end of the lake. It had grown rough since we left camp, and it did not seem to me that we could get to the point, for it meant running into the wind part of the way. It was an exciting hour's work, and the men were very quiet. There was none of the usual merry chat. Evidently a storm was coming, and unless we could pass that long, rocky point, and win the shelter of the bay beyond, we might be delayed for days. The big waves came rolling up the lake, and as each reached us the bottom of the canoe was tipped towards it a little to prevent its coming over, and George's head turned slightly to see how it was treating his charge. At the same time I could feel my fingers which were just over the edge on the other side run along the top of the water, and now and then it came over and slipped up my sleeve.

It was squally, and anxiously five pairs of eyes watched the sky and the point. It was a relief when the wind dropped a little, but then we could see it had risen again, roughening the water in the distance some minutes before it reached us. As I watched the other canoe slip down the long slope of a big wave I wondered, often, if it would come up again, for it looked as if bound straight for the bottom of the lake. Soon, however, it was on the crest of another wave and ready to dip again. The most exciting part of the experience was watching its motions. The perspective made them seem more remarkable than those of my own, which indeed were startling enough at times.

With glad hearts we felt the wind drop a little as we neared the point. Then, bending to their paddles with all the strength of their strong arms, the men carried the canoes beyond the breakers to where we could turn our backs to the wind, and we slipped into the quiet bay.

CHAPTER XI

STORM-BOUND ON MICHIKAMATS

We had not reached our haven too soon. Almost immediately the wind rose again, and by noon was blowing so strong that we could have done nothing in any part of Lake Michikamau, not to speak of crossing the upper end in a heavy south wind. Around the point I did not find things look as I expected. It was only a very shallow bay, and where we looked for the islands a long, narrow point of land stretched out from the west shore to the northeast. Flowing round the eastern end of this point was a rapid, some two hundred yards in length, and at the head of this we found a little lake, between two and three miles in length, lying northeast and southwest. All the eastern portion of it was shallow, and it was with considerable difficulty we succeeded in getting the canoes up to the low shore, where we had lunch. I wondered much if this could possibly be Michikamats, which is mapped in, in dotted lines, as a lake twenty-five miles long lying northwest.

In the afternoon my perplexities were cleared up. A small river, coming down from the northwest, flowed in at the east end of the lake. Three-quarters of a mile of poling, dragging, and lifting brought us up to another lake, and this proved to be Lake Michikamats. For half a mile or more at its lower end the lake is narrow and shoal. Its bed is a mass of jagged rocks, many of which rise so near to the surface that it was a work of art to find a way among them. A low point ran out north on our left, and from this point to the eastern shore stretched a long line of boulders rising at intervals from the water. This line marks the edge of the shallows, and beyond it the lake is deep and broad and stretches away northeast for more than eight miles of its length, when it bends to the northwest.

As we entered it we saw that the low range of wooded hills on our left formed the western boundary of the lake, and over the flat wooded shore on the right we could see the tops of big, barren hills of a range stretching northward. These are a continuation of the round-topped hills which border the east shore of Michikamau south of where the lake narrows. For some miles of our journey up northern Michikamau we could see these hills miles back from the low shoreline. Now we seemed to be turning towards them again. Beyond a point one mile and a quarter north from where we entered the lake a deep bay runs in to the east, and here the hills came into plain view though they were still far back from the shore. Their rounded tops were covered with moss, and low down on the sides dark patches showed where the green woods were.

It was a glorious afternoon, and the canoes scudded at racing pace before a heavy south wind. At a point on the east shore, six miles up the lake, I landed to take bearings. Here we found a peculiar mound of rocks along the edge of the water which proved to be characteristic of the whole shoreline of the lake. The rocks had been pushed out by the ice and formed a sort of wall, while over the wall moss and willows grew, with here and there a few stunted evergreens, the whole making an effective screen along the water's edge. Back of this were swamps and bogs with low moss-covered mounds running through them, and grown up with scattered tamarack and spruces. On the west shore the hills reached quite to the wall itself.

Behind this wall, at the point, we found a family of ptarmigan. When we appeared the mother bird tried vainly to hurry her flock away to a place of safety. Her mate flew across to an island a short distance north, leaving her alone to her task, but she and her little ones were all taken. Here the first wolf tracks we had seen on the trip were found.

After some time spent at the point it was time to camp. We crossed to the island, north, and as we landed a white-winged ptarmigan flew back to where had just been enacted one of the endless succession of wilderness tragedies. I wondered if he would not wish he had stayed to share the fate of his little family, and what he would do with himself now. It was a beautiful camping place we found. The Indians had found it too, and evidently had appreciated its beauty. There were the remains of many old camps there, well-worn paths leading from one to the other. It was the first place we had come upon which gave evidence of having been an abiding Place of some permanence. There must have been quite a little community there at one time. The prospect south, west, and north was very beautiful.

My tent was pitched in a charming nook among the spruce trees, and had a carpet of boughs all tipped with fresh green. The moss itself was almost too beautiful to cover; but nothing is quite so nice for carpet as the boughs. We were on a tiny ridge sloping to the south shore of the island, and over the screen of willows and evergreens at the water's edge, the wind came in strong enough to drive away the flies and mosquitoes, and leave one free to enjoy the beauty of the outlook. It was an ideal place to spend Sunday, and with a sigh of relief we settled into our island camp. The week had been a wonderfully interesting one; but it had also been an anxious and trying one in a few ways. I was glad to have passed Michikamau so quickly and easily. I wished it might be our good fortune to see some of the Indians.

Through the night the south wind rose to a gale, and showers of rain fell. On Sunday morning I was up at 7 A.M., and after a nice, lazy bath, luxuriously dressed myself in clean clothes. Then came a little reading from a tiny book that had been in Labrador before, and a good deal of thinking. Just after 9 A.M. I lay down to go to sleep again. I had not realised it before, but I was very tired. My eyes had closed but a moment when rat-a-tat-tat on the mixing pan announced breakfast. Joe had prepared it, and the others came straggling out one by one looking sleepy and happy, enjoying the thought of the day's rest, the more that it was the kind of day to make it impossible to travel. Returning to my tent after the meal I lay down to sleep. My head had no sooner touched the pillow than I was asleep, and did not wake till 1.30 P.M.

I could hear Gil outside preparing lunch, and went out to see how he was getting on. It was the first time he had attempted anything in the cooking line, and he looked anxious. We were to have fried cakes and tea, and Gil was cooking the fried cakes. They were not much to look at, for the wind had coated them well with ashes; but they tasted good, and the youngster looked quite relieved at the way they disappeared when we began to eat.

Michikamats was certainly very picturesque in the gale. The wind had six miles of unbroken sweep, and stirred the lake to wild commotion. Out of shelter I could scarcely stand against it. For a long time I watched two gulls trying to fly into the wind. They were very persistent and made a determined fight, but were at last compelled to give up and drop back to land. I spent nearly the whole afternoon watching the storm, running to cover only while the showers passed.

When we gathered for supper in the evening Job was holding a pot over the fire, and did not move to get his plate and cup with the rest. George gave me my plate of soup, and when I had nearly finished it Job set the pot down beside me, saying gently: "I just set this right here." In the pot were three fried cakes, crisp and hot and brown, exactly as I liked them.

There was much speculation as to what we should find at the head of Lake Michikamats, and I wondered how much scouting there would be to do to find the George River waters. If only we could see the Indians. Time was slipping away all too fast; the last week in August was not far distant, and the George River waters might not be easy to find. The days were becoming increasingly anxious for me. Our caribou meat was nearly gone, and a fresh supply of game would have been very welcome. There would be a chance to put out the nets when we reached the head of the lake, and the scouting had to be done. The nets had not yet touched the water.

In the night the wind veered to the north and a steady rain set in, which was still falling when morning came. All were up late for it was too stormy to travel, and rest still seemed very good. While eating breakfast we heard geese calling not far away, and started on a goose hunt. It did not prove very exciting, nor very fruitful of geese. They were at the head of the bay which ran in east of our island. There were a number of small islands in the bay separated by rock-strewn shallows, and having landed Job and Joe on one of the largest of these, George, Gilbert and I paddled round to the south of the group, and came out in the upper part of the bay. There just over the marsh grass at its head we saw five geese, but they saw us too, and before we could get near them were up and away. On the way back four red-throated loons, two old and two young, and a spruce partridge were taken.

It was nearly noon when we reached camp again, and the men were in the midst of preparing dinner when they caught sight of a big caribou stag swimming across to the point south of us. In such circumstances Job was indescribable. He seemed as if suddenly inspired with the energy of a flying bullet, and moved almost as silently. There was a spring for the canoe, and in much less time than it takes to tell it, the canoe was in the water with Job, Gilbert, and George plying their paddles with all their strength. As had happened before, the splendid creature almost reached the shore when a bullet dropped in front of him, and he turned back. His efforts were now no match for the swift paddle strokes that sent the canoe lightly towards him, and soon a shot from George's rifle ended the struggle. He was towed ashore, bled and gralloched, and brought to camp in the canoe.

Most of the afternoon was spent in cutting up the caribou, and putting it on a stage to dry. While they were busy with their task there came again the sound of the wild goose call. Seizing the rifles, George and Gilbert made off across the island, and soon came back with two young geese, and word that there was another there but too far out in the water for them to get it. Whereupon Job and Joe went off in the canoe, and after a short time came back with a third. This made a pretty good day's hunt. George's record was, one spruce partridge, two young geese, and one caribou.

We had young wild goose for supper that night. I think I never have tasted anything more delicious, and with hot fried cakes it made a supper fit for a king. As we ate the men talked about the calls of the wild birds.

George said: "I do like to hear a wild goose call." Certainly no one who heard him say it would doubt his word. After a little he continued: "There is another bird, too, that the Indians call 'ah-ha-way,' that I used to like so much to listen to when I was a boy. How I used to listen to that bird call. I tell you if you heard that bird call you could just sit and listen and listen. I don't know the English name for it. It is a very small duck, just a very little bird."

Speaking of the loons we had heard calling on Lake Michikamau he said: "You should hear some of the little Indian boys calling the loons. Men's voices are too strong and rough, but some of those little boys, they can do it very well. You will just see the loons come and circle round and round over them when they call."

All day long the rain had fallen steadily. I spent most of it in my tent, but the men had been out the whole day and were soaked. Having done their washing on Sunday they had no dry clothes to put on, and so slept wet that night.

CHAPTER XII

THE MIGRATING CARIBOU

Tuesday morning, August 8th, dawned clear and calm, and Gilbert came forth to light the fire, singing: "Glory, glory, hallelujah! as we go marching along." Yet before the tents were taken down the wind had sprung up from the southwest, and it was with difficulty that the canoes were launched and loaded.

A short distance above our starting-point, we were obliged to run into a sheltered bay, where part of the load was put ashore, and with the canoes thus lightened we crossed to a long, narrow point which reached half-way across from the other side, making an excellent breakwater between the upper and lower parts of the lake. The crossing was accomplished in safety, though it was rough enough to be interesting, and Job and Joe went back for what had been left behind.

The point terminated in a low, pebbly beach, but its banks farther up were ten to twelve feet high, and above it was covered with reindeer moss. Towards the outer end there were thickets of dwarf spruce, and throughout its length scattered trees that had bravely held their heads up in spite of the storms of the dread northern winter. To the south of the point was a beautiful little bay, and at its head a high sand mound which we found to be an Indian burying-place. There were four graves, one large one with three little ones at its foot, each surrounded by a neatly made paling, while a wooden cross, bearing an inscription in Montagnais, was planted at the head of each moss-covered mound. The inscriptions were worn and old except that on one of the little graves. Here the cross was a new one, and the palings freshly made. Some dis-tance out on the point stood a skeleton wigwam carpeted with boughs that were still green, and lying about outside were the fresh cut shavings telling where the Indian had fashioned the new cross and the enclosure about the grave of his little one. Back of this solitary resting-place were the moss-covered hills with their sombre forests, and as we turned from them we looked out over the bay at our feet, the shining waters of the lake, and beyond it to the blue, round-topped hills reaching upward to blend with exquisite harmony into the blue and silver of the great dome that stooped to meet them. Who could doubt that romance and poetry dwell in the heart of the Indian who chose this for the resting-place of his dead.

Walking back along the point we found it cut by caribou trails, and everywhere the moss was torn and trampled in a way that indicated the presence there of many of the animals but a short time since. Yet it did not occur to me that we might possibly be on the outskirts of the march of the migrating caribou. Ptarmigan were there in numbers, and flew up all along our way. We passed a number of old camps, one a large oblong, sixteen feet in length, with two fireplaces in it, each marked by a ring of small rocks, and a doorway at either end. Near where we landed, close in the shelter of a thicket of dwarf spruce, was a deep bed of boughs, still green, where some wandering aboriginal had spent the night without taking time or trouble to erect his wigwam, and who in passing on had set up three poles pointing northward to tell his message to whoever might come after.

68

The wind continued high, and squalls and heavy showers passed. Nevertheless, when lunch was over we pushed on, keeping close to the west shore of the lake. Little more than a mile further up the men caught sight of deer feeding not far from the water's edge. We landed, and climbing to the top of the rock wall saw a herd of fifteen or more feeding in the swamp. I watched them almost breathless. They were very beautiful, and it was an altogether new and delightful experience to me. Soon they saw us and trotted off into the bush, though without sign of any great alarm. George and Job made off across the swamp to the right to investigate, and not long after returned, their eyes blazing with excitement, to say that there were hundreds of them not far away.

Slipping hurriedly back into the canoes we paddled rapidly and silently to near the edge of the swamp. Beyond it was a barren hill, which from near its foot sloped more gradually to the water. Along the bank, where this lower slope dropped to the swamp, lay a number of stags, with antlers so immense that I wondered how they could possibly carry them. Beyond, the lower slope of the hill seemed to be a solid mass of caribou, while its steeper part was dotted over with many feeding on the luxuriant moss.

Those lying along the bank got up at sight of us, and withdrew towards the great herd in rather leisurely manner, stopping now and then to watch us curiously. When the herd was reached, and the alarm given, the stags lined themselves up in the front rank and stood facing us, with heads high and a rather defiant air. It was a magnificent sight. They were in summer garb of pretty brown, shading to light grey and white on the under parts. The horns were in velvet, and those of the stags seemed as if they must surely weigh down the heads on which they rested. It was a mixed company, for male and female were already herding together. I started towards the herd, kodak in hand, accompanied by George, while the others remained at the shore. The splendid creatures seemed to grow taller as we approached, and when we were within two hundred and fifty yards of them their defiance took definite form, and with determined step they came towards us.

The sight of that advancing army under such leadership, was decidedly impressive, recalling vivid mental pictures made by tales of the stampeding wild cattle in the west. It made one feel like getting back to the canoe, and that is what we did. As we ran towards the other men I noticed a peculiar smile on their faces, which had in it a touch of superiority. I understood in part when I turned, for the caribou had stopped their advance, and were again standing watching us. Now the others started towards the herd. Emboldened by their courage, and thinking that perhaps they held the charm that would make a close approach to the herd possible, I accompanied them. Strange to relate it was but a few minutes till we were all getting back to the canoes, and we did not again attempt to brave their battle front. We and the caribou stood watching each other for some time. Then the caribou began to run from either extreme of the herd, some round the south end of the hill, and the others away to the north, the line of stags still maintaining their position.

After watching them for some time we again entered the canoes. A short paddle carried us round the point beyond which the lake bent to the northwest, and there we saw them swimming across the lake. Three-quarters of a mile out was an island, a barren ridge standing out of the water, and from mainland to island they formed as they swam a broad unbroken bridge; from the farther end of which they poured in steady stream over the hill-top, their flying forms clearly outlined against the sky. How long we watched them I could not say, for I was too excited to take any note of time; but finally the main body had passed.

Yet when we landed above the point from which they had crossed, companies of them, eight, ten, fifteen, twenty in a herd, were to be seen in all directions. When I reached the top of the ridge accompanied by George and Gilbert, Job and Joe were already out on the next hill beyond, and Job was driving one band of a dozen or more toward the water at the foot of the hill, where some had just plunged in to swim across. Eager to secure a photo or two at closer range than any I had yet obtained, I handed George my kodak and started down the hill at a pace which threatened every second to be too fast for my feet, which were not dressed in the most appropriate running wear. However the foot of the hill was reached in safety. There a bog lay across our way. I succeeded in keeping dry for a few steps, then gave it up and splashed through at top speed. We had just hidden ourselves behind a huge boulder to wait for the coming of the herd, when turning round I saw it upon the hill from which we had just come. While exclaiming over my disappointment I was startled by a sound immediately behind me, and turning saw a splendid stag and three does not twenty feet away. They saw us and turned, and I had scarcely caught my breath after the surprise when they were many more than twenty feet away, and there was barely time to snap my shutter on them before they, disappeared over the brow of the hill.

The country was literally alive with the beautiful creatures, and they did not seem to be much frightened. The apparently wanted only to keep what seemed to them a safe distance between us, and would stop to watch us curiously within easy rifle shot. Yet I am glad I can record that not a shot was fired at them. Gilbert was wild, for he had in him the hunter's instinct in fullest measure. The trigger of Job's rifle clicked longingly, but they never forgot that starvation broods over Labrador, and that the animal they longed to shoot might some time save the life of one in just such extremity as that reached by Mr. Hubbard and his party two years before.

The enjoyment of the men showed itself in the kindling eyes and faces luminous with pleasure. All his long wilderness experience had never afforded Job anything to compare with that which this day had brought him. He was like a boy in his abandon of delight, and I am sure that if the caribou had worn tails we should have seen Job running over the hills holding fast to one of them.

Before proceeding farther we re-ascended the hill which we first climbed to take a look at the lake. It could be seen almost from end to end. The lower part which we had passed was clear, but above us the lake was a network of islands and water. The hills on either side seemed to taper off to nothing in the north, and I could see where the land appeared to drop away beyond this northern horizon which looked too near to be natural. North of Michikamats were more smaller lakes, and George showed me our probable route to look for "my river". Squalls and showers had been passing all the afternoon, and as it drew towards evening fragments of rainbow could be seen out on the lake or far away on the hills beyond it. Labrador is a land of rainbows and rainbow colours, and nowhere have I ever seen them so brilliant, so frequent and so variedly manifested. Now the most brilliant one of all appeared close to us, its end resting directly on a rock near the foot of the hill. George never knew before that there is a pot of gold at the end of the rainbow. I suspect he does not believe it yet for I could not persuade him to run to get it. Gilbert, more credulous, made a determined attempt to secure the treasure, but before he reached the rock the rainbow had moved off and carried the gold to the middle of the lake.

Camp was made a little farther up. When it was ready for the night Job and Joe were again off to watch the caribou. They were feeding on the hills and swimming back and forth from islands to mainland, now in companies, now a single caribou. Job was so near one as he came out of the water that he could have caught him by the horns. Now and then a distant shout told that Job and the caribou had come to close quarters.

While George and Gilbert prepared supper, I sat writing in my diary with feet stretched to the fire, for I was wet and it was cold that night. Suddenly I was startled to hear George exclaim in tragic tones: "Oh! look there! Isn't that too bad!"

Looking up quickly to see what was the trouble I saw him gazing regretfully at a salt shaker which he had just drawn from his pocket.

"Just see," he exclaimed, "what I've been carrying round in my pocket all the time you were running after those caribou, and never thought about it at all. Well, I am sorry for that. I could just have given you a bit and you would have been all right."

For fifty miles of our journey beyond this point we saw companies of the caribou every day, and sometimes many times a day, though we did not again see them in such numbers. The country was a network of their trails, in the woodlands and bogs cut deep into the soft soil, on the barren hillsides broad, dark bands converging to the crossing place at the river.

At the time I made my journey the general movement of the caribou was towards the east; but where they had come from or whither they were going we could not tell. Piles of white hair which we found later at a deserted camp on Cabot Lake where the Indians had dressed the skins, and the band of white hair clinging to the west bank of the George River, opposite our camp of August 15th, four feet above the then water-level, pointed to an earlier occupation of the country, while the deep cut trails and long piles of whitened antlers, found at intervals along the upper George River, all indicated that this country is favourite ground with them. Yet whether they had been continuously in this territory since the spring months or not I did not ascertain. The

Indians whom we found at Resolution Lake knew nothing of their presence so near them.

Towards the end of August the following year Mr. Cabot, while on a trip inland from Davis Inlet, on the east coast, found the caribou in numbers along the Height of Land, and when he joined the Indians there, though the great herd had passed, they had killed near a thousand. It would therefore seem not improbable that at the time I made my journey they were bending their steps in the direction of the highlands between the Atlantic and the George.

The movements of the barren ground caribou of Labrador have never been observed in the interior as they have been in the country west of Hudson Bay. So far as I can learn I alone, save the Indians, have witnessed the great migration there; but from such information as I was able to gather later at the coast, their movements appear to be as erratic as those of the caribou of northern Canada. [See Warburton Pike's "Barren Grounds of Northern Canada".]

From Mr. John Ford, the Agent of the Hudson's Bay Company's Post at the mouth of the George River, I learned that they cross in the neighbourbood of the post at different times of the year. He has seen them there in July and August, in October and November, in January, February, and March. They are seen only a few days in the summer time, but in winter stay much longer—sometimes two months. In 1903 they were near the post all through February and March. On one occasion in the summer one of Mr. Ford's Eskimo hunters went to look for caribou, and after walking nearly all day turned home, arriving shortly before midnight, but without having found a trace of deer. The next morning at three o'clock they were running about on the hills at the post in such numbers that without trouble as many could be killed as were desired.

From the George River post they hunt west for the caribou, which are more often found in the vicinity of Whale River post than at either George River or Fort Chimo to the west. For the five years preceding my visit the caribou had crossed regularly in November at Whale River. That is to say they were seen there in great numbers, but no one knew whence they had come, or whither they went. Their coming cannot, however, be counted upon every year.

In September 1889 the whole band of George River Eskimo went for the annual hunt, by which they expect to supply themselves with winter clothing. Day after day they travelled on without finding the deer. When provisions gave out they were so far away from the post that they dared not turn back. One family after another dropped behind. Finally, the last little company gave up, one young man only having the strength to go any farther. He, too, was about to sink down, when at last be came upon the caribou. He went back to help the others, but in spite of their best efforts twenty-one of the band perished from starvation.

That the caribou of Labrador have greatly decreased in numbers seems certain. Mr. Peter M'Kenzie, Chief Factor of the Hudson's Bay Company in the east, who was a fellow-traveller on my return journey, told me that many years ago while in charge of Fort Chimo he had seen the caribou passing steadily for three days just as I saw them on this 8th of August, not in thousands, but hundreds of thousands. The depletion of the great herds of former days is attributed to the unreasoning slaughter of the animals at the time of migration by Indians in the interior and Eskimo of the coast, not only at Ungava, but on the east coast as well, for the caribou sometimes find their way to the Atlantic. The fires also which have swept the country, destroying the moss on which they feed, have had their share in the work of destruction.

Only twice during the journey did we find trace of their enemy—the wolves. These hunt the caribou in packs, cutting out a single deer, and following him till his strength is gone, when they jump on him and pull him down. Mr. M'Kenzie tells how, when on one of his hunting trips at Fort Chimo, a caribou came over the ridge but a short distance from him followed by seven wolves. The animal had almost reached the limit of his strength. He ran with head low and tongue hanging out. From cover of a boulder Mr. M'Kenzie waited for them to pass, and one after another he dropped four of the wolves. The others taking the hint altered their course, and the victim escaped.

CHAPTER XIII

ACROSS THE DIVIDE

The gale continued all night with passing showers, which threatened to riddle the tent with their force, and it was not till ten the following forenoon that we were able to proceed, hugging the shore as we went. Deer were about in all directions, and as we rounded a point near the head of the lake, George, standing in the bow of the canoe, and looking across to the woods beyond the big marsh, which stretched away northward, said: "The wood over there is just moving with them."

Camp was pitched on the point among the spruce and tamarack, preparatory to scouting for George River waters, and lunch over, Job and Joe were off to the task, while George and Gilbert built a stage and put the caribou meat over the fire to smoke and dry again. It was my golden opportunity to air my camp stuff, and bags were emptied and everything spread out in the sunshine and wind. Later my washing, neglected on Sunday on account of the storm, was added to the decorations.

How very much I wanted to go scouting with Job and Joe! Here I expected difficulties in finding the way. The map I carried indicated a number of detached lakes stretching miles northward from Lake Michikamats, and to find among the lakes of this upper plain the one which should prove the source of the George River, promised to be interesting work. Inwardly impatient I waited for the return of the men. Less than two hours later I saw them come down across the marsh to where they had left the canoe. There mounting a huge boulder they sat down to watch the caribou.

This was trying, when I had so eagerly waited for the news they were to bring; but a little reflection convinced me that it meant simply—nothing definite about the George River. Otherwise they would have come immediately to camp. The conclusion proved correct, and when towards evening they came in, the report was— more streams and lakes leading northward up the slope of the plateau. We had not yet reached the real head of the Nascaupee River.

Thursday morning, August 10th, we began our portage across the marsh. Before leaving, the men had a few careless, ineffectual shots at a crow which had alighted near the camp, the first of its kind we had seen on the trip. The marsh was one mile wide from east to west, and reached almost two miles northward from the upper end of the lake. It was cut by many little streams, which, issuing from a tiny lake one mile and a half above camp, wound about among the grassy hummocks of the marsh, collecting half a mile below in a small pond, to break again into innumerable tiny channels leading down to Lake Michikamats.

The pond and streams above gave us some paddling. Then came more portaging to the little lake. Below it lay a stretch of higher ground which was a queer sort of collection of moss-covered hummocks, crisscrossed by caribou trails cut deep into the soft soil. Here cloudberries grew in abundance, and though not yet ripe, they were mature enough to taste almost as good as the green apples I used to indulge in surreptitiously in the days of my youth. They seemed a great treat now, for they were the first fruit found in abundance on the trip, though we had seen a few that were nearly ripe on an island in Lake Michikamau, and on the 8th of August Gilbert had gathered a handful of ripe blueberries on Caribou Hill.

The lake was about one mile long and two hundred yards wide, and was fed by a good-sized stream coming down from the north in continuous rapids. The stream was deep, and the canoes were poled up with all the outfit in them to the lake above, and on a great bed of huge, packed boulders at the side of the stream we halted for lunch. The quest was becoming more and more interesting. When was our climbing to end? When were we really going to find the headwaters of the Nascaupee, and stand at the summit of the plateau? It was thoroughly exciting work this climbing to the top of things.

That afternoon our journey carried us northwest through beautiful Lake Adelaide, where long wooded points and islands cutting off the view ahead, kept me in a constant state of suspense as to what was to come next. About 4 P.M. we reached the northern extremity of the lake, where the way seemed closed; but a little searching discovered a tiny stream coming in from the north and west of this the well marked Indian trail. What a glad and reassuring discovery it was, for it meant that we were on the Indian highway from Lake Michikamau to George River. Perhaps our task would not be so difficult after all.

The portage led north one hundred yards to a little lake one mile long and less than one quarter wide, and here we found ourselves at the very head of the Nascaupee River. There was no inlet to the lake, and north of it lay a bog two hundred yards wide which I knew must be the Height of Land, for beyond it stretched a body of water which had none of the appearance of a still water lake, and I felt sure we should find its waters flowing north.

It was just 5 P.M. when, three hundred miles of my journey into the great, silent wilderness passed, I stepped out of the canoe to stand at last on the summit of the Divide—the first of the white race to trace the Nascaupee River to its source.

I had a strange feeling of being at the summit of the world. The country was flat and very sparsely wooded, but I could not see far. It seemed to fall away on every hand, but especially to north and south. The line of the horizon was unnaturally near, and there was more than the usual realising sense of the great space between the earth and the sky. This was enhanced by the lifting of a far distant hill-top above the line as if in an attempt to look across the Divide.

That morning I had found myself with only a few films left, for the fascination of taking the first photographs of the region traversed had betrayed me into using my material more lavishly than I should; but now I squandered two films in celebration of the achievement, taking one picture looking out over the waters flowing South to

Lake Melville and the Atlantic and facing about, but without otherwise changing my position, one over the waters which I felt sure we should find flowing north to Ungava Bay.

In a wonderfully short time the outfit had been portaged across, and we were again in the canoes, the quest now being, not for the inlet but for the outlet of the lake, a much less difficult task. Less than an hour's paddling carried us to the point where the George River, as a tiny stream, steals away from its source in Lake Hubbard, as if trying to hide in its rocky bed among the willows, to grow in force and volume in its three hundred mile journey to Ungava, till at its discharge there it is a great river three miles in width.

Here at its beginning on the boggy margin of the stream we went into camp. Here I saw the sun set and rise again, and as I lay in my tent at dawn, with its wall lifted so that I could look out into the changing red and gold of the eastern sky, I heard a splashing of water near, and looking up saw a little company of caribou cross at the head of the stream and disappear towards the sunrise.

CHAPTER XIV

THROUGH THE LAKES OF THE UPPER GEORGE

How little I had dreamed when setting out on my journey that it would prove beautiful and of such compelling interest as I had found it. I had not thought of interest—except that of getting the work done—nor of beauty. How could Labrador be beautiful? Weariness and hardship I had looked for, and weariness I had found often and anxiety, which was not yet past in spite of what had been achieved; but of hardship there had been none. Flies and mosquitoes made it uncomfortable sometimes but not to the extent of hardship. And how beautiful it had been, with a strange, wild beauty, the remembrance of which buries itself silently in the deep parts of one's being. In the beginning there had been no response to it in my heart, but gradually in its silent way it had won, and now was like the strength-giving presence of an understanding friend. The long miles which separated me from the world did not make me feel far away—just far enough to be nice—and many times I found myself wishing I need never have to go back again. But the work could not all be done here.

Half the distance across the peninsula had been passed, and now on August 11th we were beginning the descent of the George River. Would the Labrador skies continue to smile kindly upon me? It would be almost if not quite a three hundred mile journey to Ungava, and it might be more. Could we make the post by the last week in August? The men appeared confident; but for me the days which followed held anxious hours, and the nights sleepless ones as I tried to make my decision whether in case it should become evident we could not reach Ungava in time, I should turn back, leaving the work uncompleted, or push on, accepting the consequent long winter journey back across Labrador, or round the coast, and the responsibility of providing for my four guides for perhaps a full year. At least the sun shone on the beginning of the journey, and about nine o'clock, the last pack having gone forward, I set off down the portage below Lake Hubbard, a prayer in my heart that the journey might be swift.

The prayer seemed doomed to remain unanswered at first. Before noon of that day the sun was hidden, and for nearly a week we did not again see his face. Violent storms of wind and rain and snow made progress difficult or impossible, and on August 16th we were camped only thirty miles from the Height of Land.

The upper river proved a succession of lake expansions of varying sizes, their waters dropping from one to the other down shallow rapids. At the Height of Land, and for some miles beyond, the country is flat and boggy, and sparsely wooded with tamarack and spruce, many of the tall, slender tops of the former being bent completely over by the storms. The spruce was small and scant, increasing in size and quantity as we descended from the highest levels, but nowhere on the northern slope attaining the size reached in the valley of the Nascaupee.

Gradually low, barren ridges began to appear, their white mossy sides marked by caribou trails which formed a network over the country we were passing through, and all were freshly cut with hoof marks. Every day there were herds or single deer to be seen along the way, and at a number of points we passed long piles of whitened antlers. Other game too, ducks, geese, and ptarmigan had become plentiful since we entered the caribou country, and now and then a few were taken to vary the monotony of the diet of dried caribou meat. Loons were about us at all hours, and I grew to love their weird call as much almost as the Indians do.

We travelled too fast to fish, and it was stormy, but the indications were that in places at least fish were abundant. When we ran down to the little lake, on which our camp of August 12th was pitched, hundreds of fish played at its surface, keeping the water in constant commotion. They were in no wise disturbed by our presence and would turn leisurely over within two feet of the canoe. I ran out my troll as we paddled down the lake—but not a nibble did I get. The men said they were white fish.

Every day we expected to see or hear something of the wolves which are said to attend the movements of the caribou; but no sign of them appeared, save the one track found at the point on Lake Michikamats.

Signs of the Indians became more numerous, and on a point near the head of Cabot Lake we found a camp but lately deserted, and left, evidently, with the idea of return in the near future. The Indians had been there all through the spring, and we found a strongly built cache which the men thought probably contained furs, but which we did not, of course, disturb. It was about ten feet long and six feet wide at the base, and built in the form of an A, with the trunks of trees from five to six inches in diameter set up close together and chinked with moss and boughs.

There were many of the uncovered wigwams standing about, one a large oblong with three fireplaces in it. Lying near the wigwams were old clothes of a quite civilised fashion, pots, kettles, a wooden tub, paint-cans and brushes, paddles, a wooden shovel, broken bones, piles of hair from the deer skins they had dressed, and a skin stretcher. Some steel traps hung in a tree near, and several iron pounders for breaking bones. On a stage, under two deer-skins, were a little rifle, a shot gun, and a piece of dried deer's meat. A long string of the bills of birds taken during the spring, hung on a tree near the water, and besides each of the various wigwams, in the line of them which stretched along the south shore of the point, a whitened bone was set up on a long pole for luck.

The river gradually increased in volume, and all previous excitement of work in the swift water seemed to grow insignificant when my long course in running rapids began. Perhaps it was because the experience was new, and I did not know what to expect; but as the little canoe careered wildly down the slope from one lake to the next with, in the beginning, many a scrape on the rocks of the river bed, my nervous system contracted steadily till, at the foot where we slipped out into smooth water again, it felt as if dipped into an astringent.

78

A few miles below Cabot Lake the river is joined by what we judged to be its southeast branch, almost equal to the middle river in size. This branch, together with a chain of smaller lakes east of Lake Michikamau, once formed the Indian inland route from the Nascaupee River to the George used at times of the year when Lake Michikamau was likely to be impassable on account of the storms. It had been regularly travelled in the old days when the Indians of the interior traded at Northwest River post; but since the diversion of their trade to the St. Lawrence it had fallen into disuse.

There was much talk of our prospective meeting with the Nascaupees which I did not understand; and it was not until the evening of August 14th, as I sat after supper at the camp fire, that I became conscious of the real concern with which the men were looking forward to the event.

For two precious days we had been unable to move on account of the storms. The rain had fallen steadily all day, changing to snow towards evening, and now, though the downpour had ceased, the black clouds still fled rolling and tossing over head before the gale, which roared through the spruce forest, and sent the smoke of the big camp fire whirling now this way, now that, as it found its way into our sheltered nook.

George and Joe were telling amusing stories of their boyhood experiences at Rupert's House, the pranks they played on their teacher, their fights, football, and other games, and while they talked I bestowed some special care upon my revolver. Job sat smoking his pipe, listening with a merry light in his gleaming, black eyes, and Gilbert lounged on the opposite side of the fire with open-mouthed boyish attention.

The talk drifted to stories of the Indians, tributary to Rupert's House, and the practical jokes perpetrated on them while camped about the post to which they brought each spring from the far interior their winter's catch of furs. There were stories of Hannah Bay massacre, and the retribution which followed swift and certain; and of their own trips inland, and the hospitality of the Indians. The talk ended with an anxious "If it were only the Hudson Bay Indians we were coming to, there would be no doubt about the welcome we should get."

Turning to me, George remarked, "You are giving that revolver a fine rubbing up to-night."

"Yes," I replied, laughing a little: "I am getting ready for the Nascaupees."

"They would not shoot you," he said gravely. "It would be us they would kill if they took the notion. Whatever their conjurer tells them to do, they will do."

"No," asserted Gilbert, who boasted some traditional knowledge of the Nascaupees, "they would not kill you, Mrs. Hubbard. It would be to keep you at their camp that they would kill us."

I had been laughing at George a little, but Gilbert's startling announcement induced a sudden sobriety. As I glanced from one to the other, the faces of the men were all unwontedly serious. There was a whirl of thoughts for a moment, and then I asked, "What do you think I shall be doing while they are killing you? You do not need to suppose that because I will not kill rabbits, or ptarmigan, or caribou, I should have any objection to killing a Nascaupee Indian if it were necessary."

Nevertheless the meeting with the Indians had for me assumed a new and more serious aspect, and, remembering their agony of fear lest some harm befall me ere we reached civilisation again, I realised how the situation seemed to the men. When I went to my tent, it was to lie very wide awake, turning over in my mind plans of battle in case the red men proved aggressive.

The following morning the weather was still bad but we attempted to go forward. Soon a snow squall drove us to the shelter of the woods. When it had passed we were again on the water; but rain came on and a gale of wind drove it into our faces, till they burned as if hot water instead of cold were pelting them. We could make no headway, and so put ashore on the right bank of the river to wait for calmer weather. Camp was made on a tiny moss-covered ridge of rock back of the stretch of swamp along the shore, and soon a roaring fire sent out its welcome warmth to the wet and shivering wayfarers crouching near it in the shelter of the spruce. How cold it was! And how slowly we were getting on!

The river widened here, and on the left bank, at short intervals broad trails with fresh cut tracks led down to its edge, and along the shore a wide band of white caribou hair clung to the bank four feet above the river, where it had been left by the receding water. So we knew that the caribou had been in possession of the region since shedding their winter coats.

We had been sitting by the fire only a little while when Job, who, after his usual manner had disappeared, called to us in a low, eager voice from one hundred feet away. He said only one word— "Joe"—but we all knew what it meant and there was a rush in the direction in which he had again disappeared. A herd of fifteen caribou were swimming across from the opposite shore straight to the little bay above our landing. Under cover of the woods and willows we stole down quite close to the water and waited until they came almost to shore. Then springing from our hiding places we shouted at them. The beautiful, frightened creatures turned and went bounding back through the shallow water, splashing it into clouds of spray, till they sank into the deeper tide and only heads and stubs of tails could be seen as they swam back to the other shore. They were nearly all young ones, some of them little fawns.

All day long, at short intervals, companies of them were seen crossing, some one way, some another. Towards evening two herds passed the camp at the same time, one to the east of us but a short distance away, and the other along the foot of the ridge on the west, not fifty feet from our camp.

On Wednesday, against the strong northwest wind, we succeeded in making six and a half miles, passing the mouth of the southwest branch of the Upper George River; and when at 3 P.M. we reached the head of Long Lake it was too rough to venture on, and we had to go into camp.

I felt rather desperate that night, and sick with disappointment. One week of precious time was gone, it was the 16th of the month, and we were only thirty miles, perhaps a little more, from the Height of Land. How was it possible to reach the post in time for the ship now?

"We will get you there about two days before the ship arrives," George insisted.

"When we get down below the lakes we can make forty miles a day if the weather is good," said Joe.

But I was not reassured. When we should get down below the lakes we could travel fast perhaps; but the last one, Indian House Lake, where the old Hudson's Bay Company post had been, was still far, far north of us, and no one knew what lay between. Perhaps there was a bare possibility that we might make the journey in ten days; but I knew I could not count on it. Had I a right to undertake the return journey with its perils? I was not sure.

My tent was sweet that night with the fragrance of its carpet of balsam boughs, and a big bunch of twin flowers, which grew in profusion there; but it was late before I slept. Perhaps two hours after I awoke to find a big moon peering into my face through the open front of my tent.

I was startled at first, and instinctively reached for my revolver, not knowing what it was; but when full consciousness had returned, whether it was the effect of the moon or not, the question had somehow been settled. I knew I should go on to Ungava whatever the consequences might be.

CHAPTER XV

THE MONTAGNAIS INDIANS

The night was very still when I awoke, but it was cold. Frost sparkled in the moonlight on willows and low growth, and when at first sign of dawn I reached for my stockings and duffel to put them on, they were frozen stiff. I did not wait to hunt out dry ones, but slipped them on for I was too anxious to be on the march again. I meant to go on to Ungava now, no matter what befell; *perhaps* we could yet be in time for the ship. She might be delayed.

The men were astir early, and at a quarter to six we were off. Already the lake was almost too rough again to go forward. The wind had risen, and blew cold across the water driving the morning mists before it. Now and then they lifted a little, giving a glimpse of the farther shore, or parted overhead where a patch of deep blue could be seen. It was rather shivery, but I loved it. Two hours later the mists were gone, and for the first time since leaving Lake Hubbard we saw the sun again.

It was a glorious day, the kind which almost all the eventful days of our journey had been. I wanted to compel it to yield me something of value and interest, and it did; for after we had passed down the stretch of river below Long Lake and out into the larger one which I afterwards named Resolution, we came upon the first camp of the Indians.

When we entered the lake we were surrounded by numbers of islands in its upper extremity, but beyond it was clear and stretched away northward calm and beautiful after the storm. Its shores were low for the most part, but four miles down the lake a high, sandy point reached far out from the east shore, and it was there we found the Indians.

At first, we could see only a shapeless dark mass on the hillside. It moved and swayed now this way, now that, and the first thought was that it was caribou; but when there came the flash of sunlight on metal from the midst of it, and the sound of rifle shots, there was no longer any mistaking it for caribou.

As we came towards them the firing continued at intervals, and now and then I sent back an answering shot from my revolver; but it was not without a feeling of uneasiness that we approached. I thought of many things which might happen and the men paddled very slowly; but our amusement may be imagined when, on drawing nearer, we found that they were all women and children. There was much screaming and shouting from the hill.

"Go away, go away," they shrieked. "We are afraid of you. Our husbands are away."

Their speech was that of the Montagnais Indians which George understood, having learned to speak it while at Northwest River post in the winter of 1903-1904.

"*Tanta sebo?*" (Where is the river?) shouted Job into the din, "*Tanta sebo?*"

When they ceased their screaming to listen, George called to them in Montagnais: "We are strangers and are passing through your country."

A swift change followed these few words in their own familiar tongue. There was eager talking together, the screams of terror were changed to laughter, and four of the older women ran down to the landing to welcome us. We were greeted with much handshaking, and their number was gradually swelled from the camp on the hill. They displayed not the least sign of shyness or embarrassment, being altogether at their ease. Their clothing was of a quite civilised fashion, the dresses being of woollen goods Of various colours made with plain blouse and skirt, while on their feet they wore moccasins of dressed deerskin. The jet black hair was parted from forehead to neck, and brought round on either side, where it was wound into a little hard roll in front of the ear and bound about with pieces of plain cloth or a pretty beaded band. Each head was adorned with a *tuque* made from black and red broadcloth, with beaded or braided band around the head. Both the manner of wearing the hair and the *tuque* were exceedingly picturesque and becoming, and the types were various as those to be found in other communities, ranging from the sweet and even beautiful face to the grossly animal like. They were not scrupulously clean, but were not dirtier than hundreds of thousands to be found well within the borders of civilisation, and all, even the little children, wore the crucifix.

Their men had gone down to Davis Inlet, on the east coast, to trade for winter supplies. They had been away five days and were expected to return soon, the outward trip being made in three or four days while the return requires five. The camp was now eagerly awaiting the arrival of the tea, sugar, and tobacco, the new gowns, the gay shawls and the trinkets which make the return from the post the great event of the year.

As their speech indicated, these people were found to belong to the Montagnais tribe, which is a branch of the Cree Nation, and is tributary to the posts along the St. Lawrence. There after the winter's hunt they gather in hundreds at Mingan and Seven Islands, and it is then they receive from the Roman Catholic missionaries instruction in the Christian faith. This camp, the only one of the tribe to do so, had for some years traded at Davis Inlet, on the northeast coast. We could gather little from the women about the route to Davis Inlet further than that it is a difficult one, and for this reason they do not accompany the hunters on the yearly journey there.

The "Mush-a-wau e-u-its" (Barren Grounds people), the Nascaupee Indians, whom Mr. Hubbard had been so eager to visit, and who also are a branch of the Cree Nation, they informed us, have their hunting grounds farther down the river.

"You will sleep twice before coming to their camp," they said.

We were assured of a friendly reception there, for the two camps are friendly and sometimes visit each other; but they could tell us little about the river, because in making the journey between the two camps, they use a portage route through lakes to the east of the river. The journey to the George River post at Ungava they thought would take two months.

My heart sank as this was interpreted to me. In that case I could no longer entertain any hope of being in time for the ship. It would mean, too, the entire journey back in winter weather. I had counted that even if we missed the ship we could probably reach Lake Michikamau on the return before winter set in; but that also would be impossible. In the midst of the sickening feeling of disappointment and uncertainty which came with this information, I was conscious of being thankful that the main question had been decided.

Rather disconsolately I went up for a brief look at the camp on the hill. The situation was beautiful, and commanded a view from end to end of Resolution Lake, which extended about four miles both north and south of the point, and was divided into two distinct parts, just opposite the camp, by a long island with points of land reaching towards it from north and south. Beyond the island lay a broad sheet of water which seemed equal in size to the one we were on, and along its farther shore low blue ridges stretched away northward.

The skies seemed trying to make reparation for the week of storms, and the mood of the camp corresponded with that of the day. Children played about quietly, or clung to their mothers' skirts, as they watched the strangers with curious interest and the mothers were evidently happy in their motherhood as mothers otherwise.

"We are poor," said one, "and we live among the trees, but we have our children."

The camp consisted of two wigwams, one a large oblong and the other round. They were covered with dressed deer-skins drawn tight over the poles, blackened round the opening at the top by the smoke of the fires, which are built in the centre within. I was not invited to go into the wigwams, but through the opening which served as doorway in front of one of them I had a glimpse of the interior. It seemed quite orderly and clean. Four rifles, which lay on the carpet of balsam boughs, looked clean and well cared for. The dishes, pans, tea-pots, *etc.*, which were mostly of white enamel, with some china of an ordinary sort, were clean and shining. Long strings of dressed deerskin, and a few moccasins hung from the poles round the opening at the top. The moccasins were not decorated in any way, nor were those worn by the women, and I saw no sign of ornamentation of any kind, save the toques with their beaded or braided bands, and the bands on the hair.

Except for their children they were poor indeed now, for there was not a taste of sugar, tea, or tobacco at the camp. They rarely have flour, which with them is not one of the necessities of life. They were living on what fish they could catch while the hunters were away, and were not having the best success with their fishing. They did not know of the presence of the caribou so near them, and I thought regretfully of how easily we could have brought down one or more had we known of their need, and where we should find them.

Some six or eight splendid Eskimo dogs prowled about snarling at one another, and occasionally indulging in an ugly fight, at which there was a rush for clubs or tent poles to separate them; for unless separated they never stop till the one that goes down is killed. At whatever hour of the day or night a fight begins, the dogs have to, be separated, otherwise one or more of the number will be lost; and the loss of a dog is a calamity in the north country.

While I wandered over the hillside a little, keeping a wary eye on the dogs, the women devoted their attentions to the men. They were anxious to have the visit prolonged, and every inducement was held out even to offering them wives, temporary, if they would remain; but after taking a few pictures, for which they posed easily and without sign of self-consciousness, I bade them farewell and we returned to the canoes. They did not accompany us to the landing.

With the prospect of so long a journey before me I had to resist the impulse to share my provisions with them; but before we left, George carried a few ounces of tea up the hill. There was a merry chase as each tried to possess herself of the treasure. They were like children in their delight. A pair of moccasins was offered in return; but the gift of tea was too slight and they were not accepted. Soon we were slipping slowly away towards the river with an occasional glance back to the group on the hill. When a few rods from shore, Job, who had the faculty of making his English irresistibly funny whenever he chose, stood up in the stern of the canoe, and taking off his hat to them with a very elaborate bow called, "Good-bye, good-bye, my lady."

The directions we had received enabled us to find the river without difficulty, and passing down through a succession of small expansions with low, swampy shores where the wood growth was almost altogether tamarack, we camped in the evening ten miles below Resolution Lake, at the point where the river drops down through three rocky gorges to flow with strong, swift current in a distinct valley.

The lakes of the upper country were here left behind, and when we resumed our journey the following morning it was to be carried miles on a current in which the paddles were needed only for steering. Stretches of quiet water were succeeded by boisterous rapids, and sometimes I walked to lighten the canoe where the rapid was shallow. Tributaries entered on either hand, the river increased in force and volume, and when we halted for lunch some ten miles below Canyon Camp, the George had come to be a really great river.

We were getting down to the hills now and the country, which had been burned over, was exceedingly barren and desolate. On the slopes, which had been wooded, the grey and blackened tree trunks were still standing like armies of skeletons, and through their ranks the hills of everlasting rock showed grey and stern, stripped even of their covering of reindeer moss. Heavy showers passed during the day, but it was otherwise beautiful and we made good progress. When we camped that evening below Thousand Island Expansion it was with twenty-two miles to our credit.

It seemed very fine to have another good day's work behind and I felt less heavy hearted. Some thinking had convinced me that the two months' estimate for the journey to Ungava was far from correct; but I still feared it was useless to entertain hope of being in time for the ship. Yet one does hope even when it is plainly useless. Nevertheless life had come to be a serious matter with us all now, excepting Gilbert, for the men too were averse to spending a winter in Labrador, and had rather advocated a return by way of Davis Inlet or the Grand River. Gilbert alone sang and laughed as merrily as ever, undisturbed by doubts or fears.

That evening the sunset was of clear gold and the sudden chill, which in Labrador always follows, sent me shivering to the camp fire where, below the bank, on the solid, smooth-worn rock of the river-bed, we had supper of ptarmigan. But neither hunger nor perplexities could shut out the impress of the desolate grandeur of our surroundings. This was the wilderness indeed with only the crystal river and the beautiful skies to make it glad. Only? Or was there more? Or was it glad? Perhaps, yes surely, somewhere within it there was gladness; but everywhere it was beautiful with the beauty which alone, to some hearts, can carry the "still small voice." If only it would never say, "What dost thou here?" One must wish to stay and listen to it always.

Through the stillness came up the sound of the rapids below our camp. Above, fish jumped in the quiet waters where the after-glow in the sky was given back enriched and deepened. Then came night and the stars—bright northern lights—bright moon—shadows on the tent—dreams.

A ptarmigan whirred up, from the corner of my tent and I awoke to find the sun shining and everything outside sparkling with frost. The men had already begun portaging, for below camp the rapids were too heavy to take the outfit down; but when breakfast was over and the last load had been taken forward over the half-mile portage, the canoes were run down the river.

A short distance below, the river drops rapidly round many little islands of pink and white rock by a succession of picturesque falls and rapids and chutes extending for more than a mile and here a number of short portages were made. We reached the last of the islands shortly before eleven o'clock and then landed to climb a hill to the east. It rose six hundred and thirty feet above the river, but the view from the top afforded us little satisfaction so far as the route was concerned. The river could be seen for only a few miles ahead, flowing away to the northwest towards higher hills, where we could see patches of snow lying. Some miles to the east was a large lake, its outlet, a river of considerable size, joining the George River three-quarters of a mile north of where we had left the canoes. Below the junction there were many Indian signs along the shores, and we knew that there the portage route of which the Montagnais women had spoken, must lead to the river again. Steadily through the afternoon we approached the higher hills, ever on the watch for the Nascaupee camp; but we did not find it.

There was a short lift over a direct drop of four or five feet, and two portages of about half a mile past heavy rapids, at the second of which the river drops fifty feet to flow between high, sandy banks, the hills on either side standing back from the river, their broken faces red with a coating of iron rust. The intervening spaces were strewn with boulders of unusual size.

Fresh caribou tracks, the only ones seen since leaving the head of Long Lake, were found on the first portage, and on the second I gathered my first moss berries. A heavy shower passed late in the afternoon and the sky remained overcast; but we were not delayed, and towards evening arrived at the point, twenty miles below Thousand Island Expansion, where a large tributary comes in from the west, and the George River turns abruptly northward among the higher hills.

The proposal to go into camp had already been made when George discovered some ptarmigan high up the bank. There was a brisk hunt and eleven were taken. So again we supped on ptarmigan that night. I took mine in my tent on account of the mosquitoes, which were so thick that, as George expressed it, it was like walking in a snowstorm to move about outside.

CHAPTER XVI

THE BARREN GROUND PEOPLE

On Sunday morning, August 20th, I awoke in a state of expectancy. We had slept three times since leaving the Montagnais camp, and unless the Barren Grounds People were not now in their accustomed camping place, we ought to see them before night. Many thoughts came of how greatly Mr. Hubbard had wished to see them, and what a privilege he would have thought it to be able to visit them.

It seemed this morning as if something unusual must happen. It was as if we were coming into a hidden country. From where the river turned into the hills it flowed for more than a mile northward through what was like a great magnificent corridor, leading to something larger beyond.

When Joe and Gilbert, who were usually the first to get off, slipped away down the river, I realized how swift flowing the water must be. It looked still as glass and very dark, almost black. The quiet surface was disturbed only by the jumping of the fish. We saw the canoe push off and turned to put a few last touches to the loading of our own. When we looked again they were already far away. Soon, however, we had caught them up and together the two canoes ran out into the widening of the river. Here it bent a little to the northeast, but two miles farther on it again bore away to the north. In the distance we could see the mountain tops standing far apart and knew that there, between them, a lake must lie. Could it be Indian House Lake, the Mush-au-wau-ni-pi, or "Barren Grounds Water," of the Indians? We were still farther south than it was placed on the map I carried. Yet we had passed the full number of lakes given in the map above this water. Even so I did not believe it could be the big lake I had been looking forward to reaching so eagerly.

As we paddled on at a rather brisk rate I sat thinking how beautiful the river, the mountains, and the morning were. I had not settled myself to watch seriously for the Nascaupee camp, when suddenly George exclaimed, "There it is."

There it was indeed, a covered wigwam, high up on a sandy hill, which sloped to the water's edge, and formed the point round which the river flowed to the lake among the mountains. Soon a second wigwam came in sight. We could see no one at the camp at first. Then a figure appeared moving about near one of the wigwams. It was evident that they were still unconscious of our presence; but as we paddled slowly along the figure suddenly stopped, a whole company came running together, and plainly our sudden appearance was causing great excitement. There was a hurried moving to and fro and after a time came the sound of two rifle shots. I replied with my revolver. Again they fired and I replied again. Then more shots from the hill.

As we drew slowly near, the men ran down towards the landing, but halted above a narrow belt of trees near the water's edge. There an animated discussion of the newcomers took place.

We all shouted, "Bo Jou! Bo Jou!" (Bon Jour).

A chorus of Bo Jous came back from the hill.

George called to them in Indian, "We are strangers and are passing through your country."

The sound of words in their own tongue reassured them and they ran down to the landing. As we drew near we could hear them talking. I, of course, could not understand a word of it, but I learned later from George what they said.

"Who are they?"

"See the man steering looks like an Indian."

"That surely is an Indian."

"Why, there is an English woman."

"Where have they come from?"

As the canoe glided towards the landing, one, who was evidently the chief, stepped forward while the others remained a little apart. Putting out his hand to catch the canoe as it touched the sand he said, "Of course you have some tobacco?"

"Only a little," George replied. "We have come far."

Then the hand was given in greeting as we slipped ashore.

It was a striking picture they made that quiet Sabbath morning, as they stood there at the shore with the dark green woods behind them and all about them the great wilderness of rock and river and lake. You did not see it all, but you felt it. They had markedly Indian faces and those of the older men showed plainly the battle for life they had been fighting. They were tall, lithe, and active looking, with a certain air of self-possession and dignity which almost all Indians seem to have. They wore dressed deer-skin breeches and moccasins and over the breeches were drawn bright red cloth leggings reaching from the ankle to well above the knee, and held in place by straps fastened about the waist. The shirts, some of which were of cloth and some of dressed deer-skin, were worn outside the breeches and over these a white coat bound about the edges with blue or red. Their hair was long and cut straight round below the ears, while tied about the head was a bright coloured kerchief. The faces were full of interest. Up on the hill the women and children and old men stood watching, perhaps waiting till it should appear whether the strangers were friendly or hostile.

"Where did you come into the river?" the chief asked. George explained that we had come the whole length of the river, that we had come into it from Lake Michikamau, which we reached by way of the Nascaupee. He was greatly surprised. He had been at Northwest River and knew the route. Turning to the others he told them of our long journey. Then they came forward and gathered eagerly about us. We told them we were going down the river to the post at Ungava.

"Oh! you are near now,", they said. "You will sleep only five times if you travel fast."

My heart bounded as this was interpreted to me, for it meant that we should be at the post before the end of August, for this was only the twentieth. There was still a chance that we might be in time for the ship.

"Then where is the long lake that is in this river?" George enquired.

"It is here," the chief replied.

We enquired about the river. All were eager to tell about it, and many expressive gestures were added to their words to tell that the river was rapid all the way. An arm held at an angle showed what we were to expect in the rapids and a vigorous drop of the hand expressed something about the falls. There would be a few portages but they were not long, and in some places it would be just a short lift over; but it was all rapid nearly.

"And when you come to a river coming in on the other side in quite a fall you are not far from the post."

There was a tightening in my throat as I thought, "What if I had decided to turn back rather than winter in Labrador!"

"Did you see any Indians?" the chief asked.

"Yes, we have slept three times since we were at their camp."

"Were they getting any caribou?" was the next eager question. "Had they seen any signs of the crossing?" George told them of the great numbers we had seen and there followed an earnest discussion among themselves as to the probability of the caribou passing near them.

"Are you going up?" we enquired.

They replied, "No, not our country."

There were enquiries as to which way the caribou were passing, and again they talked among themselves about their hopes and fears. We learned that only three days before they had returned from Davis Inlet where they go to trade for supplies as do the Montagnais. They had come back from their long journey sick at heart to meet empty handed those who waited in glad anticipation of this the great event of the year—the return from the post. The ship had not come, and the post store was empty.

As they talked, the group about the canoe was growing larger. The old men had joined the others together with a few old women. As the story of their disappointment was told one old man said, "You see the way we live and you see the way we dress. It is hard for us to live. Sometimes we do not get many caribou. Perhaps they will not cross our country. We can get nothing from the Englishman, not even ammunition. It is hard for us to live."

All summer they had been taking an occasional caribou, enough for present needs, but little more than that, and the hunters on their return from the coast found the hands at home as empty as their own. Now the long winter stretched before them with all its dread possibilities.

We enquired of them how far it was to the coast, and found that they make the outward journey in five days, and the return trip in seven. They informed us that they had this year been accompanied part of the way in by an Englishman. All white men are Englishmen to them. As George interpreted to me, he said, "That must be Mr. Cabot."

Instantly the chief caught at the name and said, "Cabot? Yes, that is the man. He turned back two days' journey from here. He was going away on a ship."

When during the winter I had talked with Mr. Cabot of my trip he had said, "Perhaps we shall meet on the George next summer." Now I felt quite excited to think how near we had come to doing so. How I wished he had sent me a line by the Indians. I wanted to know how the Peace Conference was getting on. I wondered at first that he had not done so; but after a little laughed to myself as I thought I could guess why. How envious he would be of me, for I had really found the home camp of his beloved Nascaupees.

Meanwhile the old women had gathered about me begging for tobacco. I did not know, of course, what it was they wanted, and when the coveted tobacco did not appear they began to complain bitterly, "She is not giving us any tobacco. See, she does not want to give us any tobacco."

George explained to them that I did not smoke and so had no tobacco to give them, but that I had other things I could give them. Now that we were so near the post I could spare some of my provisions for the supply was considerably more than we should now need to take us to our journey's end. There was one partly used bag of flour which was lifted out of the canoe and laid on the beach. Then Job handed me the tea and rice bags. Two, not very clean, coloured silk handkerchiefs were spread on the beach when I asked for something to put the tea and rice in, and a group of eager faces bent over me as I lifted the precious contents from the bags, leaving only enough tea to take us to the post, and enough rice for one more pudding. An old tin pail lying near was filled with salt, and a piece of bacon completed the list. A few little trinkets were distributed among the women and from the expression on their faces, I judged they had come to the conclusion that I was not so bad after all, even though I did not smoke a pipe and so could not give them any of their precious "Tshishtemau."

Meantime I had been thinking about my photographs. Taking up one of my kodaks I said to the chief that I should like to take his picture and motioned him to stand apart. He seemed to understand quite readily and stepped lightly to one side of the little company in a way which showed it was not a new experience to him. They had no sort of objection to being snapped, but rather seemed quite eager to pose for me.

Then came an invitation to go up to the camp. As George interpreted he did not look at all comfortable, and when he asked if I cared to go I knew he was wishing very much that I would say "No," but I said, "Yes, indeed." So we went up while the other three remained at the canoes.

Even in barren Labrador are to be found little touches that go to prove human nature the same the world over. One of the young men, handsomer than the others, and conscious of the fact, had been watching me throughout with evident interest. He was not only handsomer than the others, but his leggings were redder. As we walked up towards the camp he went a little ahead, and to one side managing to watch for the impression he evidently expected to make. A little distance from where we landed was a row of bark canoes turned upside down. As we passed them be turned and, to make sure that those red leggings should not fail of their mission, be put his foot up on one of the canoes, pretending, as I passed, to tie his moccasin, the while watching for the effect.

It was some little distance up to camp. When we reached it we could see northward down the lake for miles. It lay, like a great, broad river guarded on either side by the mountains. The prospect was very beautiful. Everywhere along the way we found their camping places chosen from among the most beautiful spots, and there seemed abundant evidence that in many another Indian breast dwelt the heart of Saltatha, Warburton Pike's famous guide, who when the good priest had told him of the beauties of heaven said, "My Father, you have spoken well. You have told me that heaven is beautiful. Tell me now one thing more. Is it more beautiful than the land of the musk ox in summer, when sometimes the mist blows over the lakes, and sometimes the waters are blue, and the loons call very often? This is beautiful, my Father. If heaven is more beautiful I shall be content to rest there till I am very old."

The camp consisted of two large wigwams, the covers of which were of dressed deer-skins sewed together and drawn tight over the poles, while across the doorway hung an old piece of sacking. The covers were now worn and old and dirty-grey in colour save round the opening at the top, where they were blackened by the smoke from the fire in the centre of the wigwam.

Here the younger women and the children were waiting, and some of them had donned their best attire for the occasion of the strangers' visit. Their dresses were of cotton and woollen goods. Few wore skin clothes, and those who did had on a rather long skin shirt with hood attached, but under the shirt were numerous cloth garments. Only the old men and little children were dressed altogether in skins. One young woman appeared in a gorgeous purple dress, and on her head the black and red *tuque* with beaded band worn by most of the Montagnais women, and I wondered if she had come to the Nascaupee camp the bride of one of its braves. There was about her an air of conscious difference from the others, but this was unrecognised by them. The faces here were not bright and happy looking as at the Montagnais camp. Nearly all were sad and wistful. The old women seemed the brightest of all and were apparently important people in the camp. Even the little children's faces were sad and old in expression as if they too realised something of the cares of wilderness life.

At first they stood about rather shyly watching me, with evident interest, but making no move to greet or welcome me. I did not know how best to approach them. Then seeing a young mother with her babe in her arms standing among the group, near one of the wigwams, I stepped towards her, and touching the little bundle I spoke to her of her child and she held it so that I might see its face. It was a very young baby, born only the day before, I learned later, and the mother herself looked little more than a child. Her face was pale, and she looked weak and sick. Though she held her child towards me there was no lighting up of the face, no sign of responsive interest. Almost immediately, however, I was surrounded by nearly the whole community of women who talked rapidly about the babe and its mother.

The little creature had no made garments on, but was simply wrapped about with old cloths leaving only its face and neck bare. The outermost covering was a piece of plaid shawl, and all were held tightly in place by a stout cord passing round the bundle a number of times. It would be quite impossible for the tiny thing to move hand or foot or any part of its body except the face. As one might expect it wore an expression of utter wretchedness though it lay with closed eyes making no sound. I could make almost nothing of what they said, and when I called George to interpret for me they seemed not to want to talk.

Taking out my kodaks I set about securing a few photographs. Already the old women were beginning to prepare for the feast they were to have. Two large black pots that stood on three legs were set out, and one of the women went into the tent and brought out a burning brand to light the fire under them. Soon interest was centred in the pots. I had a little group ranged up in front of one of the wigwams, when the lady in purple, whose attention for a time had been turned to the preparations for the feast, seeing what was taking place came swiftly across and placed herself in the very centre of the group. All apparently understood what was being done and were anxious to be in the picture.

During the stay at camp I saw little sign of attempt at ornamentation. The moccasins and skin clothing I saw were unadorned. There was but the one black and red *tuque* with braided band, and the chief's daughter alone wore the beaded band on her hair, which was arranged as that of the women in the Montagnais camp. One woman coveted a sweater I wore. It was a rather bright green with red cuffs and collar, and the colour had greatly taken her fancy. I wished that I had been able to give it to her, but my wardrobe was as limited as I dared to have it, and so I was obliged to refuse her request. In a way which I had not in the least expected I found these people appealing to me, and myself wishing that I might remain with them for a time, but I could not risk a winter in Labrador for the sake of the longer visit, even had I been able to persuade the men to remain.

Already George was showing his anxiety to get away and I realised that it was not yet certain we should be in time for the ship. It might easily be more than five days to the post. I could not know how far the Indian mind had been influenced in gauging the distance by a desire to reduce to the smallest possible limit the amount of tobacco the men would need to retain for their own use. It was not far from the last week in August. Now I felt that not simply a day but even an hour might cost me a winter in Labrador.

When the word went forth that we were about to leave, all gathered for the parting. Looking about for something which I might carry away with me as a souvenir of the visit, my eyes caught the beaded band, which the chief's daughter wore on her hair, and stepping towards her I touched it to indicate my wish. She drew sharply away and said something in tones that had a plainly resentful ring. It was, "That is mine." I determined not to be discouraged and made another try. Stretched on a frame to dry was a very pretty deer-skin and I had George ask if I might have that. That seemed to appeal to them as a not unreasonable request, and they suggested that I should take one already dressed. The woman who had wanted my sweater went into the wigwam and brought out one. It was very pretty and beautifully soft and white on the inside. She again pleaded for the sweater, and as I could not grant her request I handed her back the skin; but she bade me keep it. They gave George a piece of deer-skin dressed without the hair, "to line a pair of mits," they said.

As they stood about during the last few minutes of our stay, the chief's arm was thrown across his little daughter's shoulders as she leaned confidingly against him. While the parting words were being exchanged he was engaged in a somewhat absent-minded but none the less successful, examination of her head. Many of the others were similarly occupied. There was no evidence of their being conscious that there was anything extraordinary in what they were doing, nor any attempt at concealing it. Apparently it was as much a matter of course as eating.

When I said, "Good-bye," they made no move to accompany me to the canoe.

94

"Good-bye," said George. "Send us a fair wind."

Smilingly they assured him that they would. In a minute we were in the canoe and pushing off from shore. As we turned down the lake, all eager to be shortening the distance between us and the post, I looked back. They were still standing just as we had left them watching us. Taking out my handkerchief I waved it over my head. Instantly the shawls and kerchiefs flew out as they waved a response, and with this parting look backward to our wilderness friends we turned our faces to Ungava.

CHAPTER XVII

THE RACE FOR UNGAVA

Five days to Ungava!

Seated in' the canoe with time to think I could not seem to realise the situation. Indian House Lake! Five days to Ungava! Oh! how I wanted it to be true. Ungava, in spite of hopes and resolves, had seemed always far away, mysterious, and unattainable, but now it had been suddenly thrust forward almost within my reach. If true, this would mean the well-nigh certain achievement of my heart's desire—the completion of my husband's work. Yet there were the rapids, where the skill and judgment of the men were our safeguards. One little miscalculation and it would take but an instant to whelm us in disaster. Still we had come so far on the way with success, surely it would be given to us to reach the goal in safety. But here inevitably thought flew to one who had been infinitely worthy but who had been denied.

Five days to Ungava! and because I so much wished it to be true I was afraid, for the hard things of life will sometimes make cowards of its pilgrims.

The Barren Grounds Water was very fair in the morning sunshine. It was as if, while exploring some great ruin, we had chanced into a secret, hidden chamber, the most splendid of them all, and when after lunch the promised fair wind sprang up, and the canoes with well-filled sails were speeding northward, the lake and its guardian hills became bluer and more beautiful than ever.

Nowhere did we find the lake more than two miles wide. Long points reaching out from either shore cut off the view and seemed to change the course; but in reality they did not, for it was always northward. To right and left there were the hills, now barren altogether, or again with a narrow belt of "greenwoods"—spruce, balsam, tamarack—along the shore. In many places skeleton wigwams marked the site of old Nascaupee camps. The hills on the east in places rose abruptly from the water, but on the west they stood a little back with sand-hills on terraces between and an occasional high, wedge-shaped point of sand and loose rock reached almost halfway across the lake. Often as I looked ahead, the lake seemed to end; but, the distant point passed, it stretched on again into the north till with repetition of this experience, it began to seem as if the end would never come. Streams entered through narrow openings between the hills, or roared down their steep sides. At one point the lake narrowed to about a quarter of a mile in width where the current was very swift. Beyond this point we saw the last caribou of the trip.

It was a three-year-old doe. She stood at the shore watching us curiously as we came towards her. Then stepping daintily in, she began to swim across. We soon caught her up and after playing round her in the canoe for a time the men with shouts of laughter headed her inshore and George, in the bow, leaning over caught her by the tail and we were towed merrily in the wake. Every minute I expected the canoe to turn over. However, George was soon obliged to relinquish his hold for the doe's feet touched bottom and in a moment she was speeding up the steep hillside stopping now and then to look back with wondering frightened eyes at the strange creatures she had so unexpectedly encountered.

Here where the caribou were rare, George River mosquitoes made life miserable for us. The flies, which in the Nascaupee country had been such a trial to me, had not driven the men to the use of their veils except on rare occasions; but now they were being worn even out on the lake where we were still tormented. Backs and hats were brown with the vicious wretches where they would cling waiting for a lull in the wind to swarm about our heads in such numbers that even their war song made one shiver and creep. They were larger by far than any Jersey mosquitoes ever dreamed of being, and their bite was like the touch of a live coal. Sometimes in the tent a continual patter on the roof as they flew against it sounded like a gentle rain.

The foot of the lake was finally reached on Monday evening, August 21st, at sunset, and we went into camp fifty-five to sixty miles from where we had entered it, and within sound of the first pitch in the one hundred and thirty miles of almost continuous rapids over which we were to travel. That night Job had a dream of them. He believed in dreams a little and it troubled him. He thought we were running in rapids which were very difficult, and becoming entrapped in the currents were carried over the brink of a fall. In the morning he told his dream, and the others were warned of danger ahead. My canoe was to lead the way with George in the bow and Job in the stern, while Joe and Gilbert were to follow close behind. When we left our camp an extra paddle was placed within easy reach of each canoe man so that should one snap at a critical moment another could instantly replace it.

This was a new attitude towards the work ahead and as we paddled slowly in the direction of the outlet where the hills drew together, as if making ready to surround and imprison us, my mind was full of vague imaginings concerning the river.

Far beyond my wildest thought, however, was the reality. Immediately at the outlet the canoes were caught by the swift current and for five days we were carried down through almost continuous rapids. There were long stretches of miles where the slope of the river bed was a steep gradient and I held my breath as the canoe shot down at toboggan pace. There was not only the slope down the course of the river but where the water swung past long points of loose rocks, which reach out from either shore, a distinct tilt from one side to the other could be seen, as when an engine rounds a bend. There were foaming, roaring breakers where the river flowed over its bed of boulder shallows, or again the water was smooth and apparently motionless even where the slope downward was clearly marked.

Standing in the stern of the canoe, guiding it with firm, unerring hand, Job scanned the river ahead, choosing out our course, now shouting his directions to George in the bow, or again to Joe and Gilbert as they followed close behind. Usually we ran in the shallow water near shore where the rocks of the river bed looked perilously near the surface. When the sun shone, sharp points and angles seemed to reach up into the curl of the waves, though in reality they did not, and often it appeared as if we were going straight to destruction as the canoe shot towards them. I used to wish the water were not so crystal clear, so that I might not see the rocks for I seemed unable to accustom myself to the fact that it was not by seeing the rocks the men chose the course but by the way the water flowed.

Though our course was usually in shallow water near the shore, sometimes for no reason apparent to me, we turned out into the heavier swells of the deeper stronger tide. Then faster, and faster, and faster we flew, Job still standing in the stern shouting his directions louder and louder as the roar of the rapid increased or the way became more perilous, till suddenly, I could feel him drop into his seat behind me as the canoe shot by a group of boulders, and George bending to his paddle with might and main turned the bow inshore again. Quick as the little craft had won out of the wild rush of water pouring round the outer end of this boulder barrier, Job was an his feet again as we sped onward, still watching the river ahead that we might not become entrapped. Sometimes when it was possible after passing a particularly hard and dangerous place we ran into a quiet spot to watch Joe and Gilbert come through. This was almost more exciting than coming through myself.

But more weird and uncanny than wildest cascade or rapid was the dark vision which opened out before us at the head of Slanting Lake. The picture in my memory still seems unreal and mysterious, but the actual one was as disturbing as an evil dream.

Down, down, down the long slope before us, to where four miles away Hades Hills lifted an uncompromising barrier across the way, stretched the lake and river, black as ink now under leaden sky and shadowing hills. The lake, which was three-quarters of a mile wide, dipped not only with the course of the river but appeared to dip also from one side to the other. Not a ripple or touch of white could be seen anywhere. All seemed motionless as if an unseen hand had touched and stilled it. A death-like quiet reigned and as we glided smoothly down with the tide we could see all about us a soft, boiling motion at the surface of this black flood, which gave the sense of treachery as well as mystery. As I looked down the long slope to where the river appeared to lose itself into the side of the mountain it seemed to me that there, if anywhere, the prophecy of Job's dream must be fulfilled. Cerberus might easily be waiting for us there. He would have scarcely time to fawn upon us till we should go shooting past him into the Pit.

But after all the river was not shallow up in the mountain. It only turned to the west and swifter than ever, we flew down with its current, no longer smooth and dark, but broken into white water over a broader bed of smooth-worn boulders, till three miles below we passed out into a quiet expansion, where the tension relaxed and with minds at ease we could draw in long, satisfying breaths.

The travelling day was a short one during this part of the trip, and I wondered often how the men stood the strain. Once I asked Job if running rapids did not tire him very much. He answered, "Yes," with a smile and look of surprise that I should understand such a thing.

The nights were made hideous by the mosquitoes, and I slept little. The loss of sleep made rapid running trying, and after a particularly bad night I would sit trembling with excitement as we raced down the slope. It was most difficult to resist the impulse to grasp the sides of the canoe, and to compel myself instead to sit with hands clasped about my knee, and muscles relaxed so that my body might lend itself to the motion of the canoe. Sometimes as we ran towards the west the river glittered so in the afternoon sunshine that it was impossible to tell what the water was doing. This made it necessary to land now and again, so that Job might go forward and look over the course. As the bow of the canoe turned inshore, the current caught the stern and whirled it round with such force and suddenness, that only the quick setting of a paddle on the shoreward side kept the little craft from being dashed to pieces against the rocks.

On Thursday, August 24th, I wrote in my diary: "Such a nice sleep last night albeit blankets and 'comfortable' so wet (the stopper of my hot-water bottle had not been properly screwed in the night before and they were soaked). Beautiful morning. Mountains ahead standing out against the clear sky with delicate clouds of white mist hanging along their sides or veiling the tops. One just at the bend is very, very fine. It reminds me of an Egyptian pyramid. Job is not feeling well this morning and it bothers me. I asked him if it were too many rapids. He smiled and said, 'I don't know,' but as if he thought that might be the trouble.

"Later.—Just a little below our camp we found a river coming in with a wild rush from the east. It was the largest we had yet seen and we wondered if our reckoning could be so far out that this might be the river not far from the post of which the Nascaupees had told us. Then so anxious for the noon observation and so glad to have a fine day for it. Result 57 degrees, 43 minutes, 28 seconds. That settled it, but all glad to be rapidly lessening the distance between us and Ungava.

"After noon, more rapids and I got out above one of them to walk. I climbed up the river wall to the high, sandy terrace above. This great wall of packed boulders is one of the most characteristic features of the lower river. It is thrown up by the action of ice in the spring floods, and varies all the way from twenty feet at its beginning to fifty and sixty feet farther down. One of the remarkable things about it is that the largest boulders lie at the top, some of them so huge as to weigh tons. On the terrace, moss berries and blue berries were so thick as to make walking slippery. The river grows more magnificent all the time. I took one photograph of the sun's rays slanting down through a rift in the clouds, and lighting up the mountains in the distance. I am feeling wretched over not having more films. How I wish I had brought twice as many.

"While running the rapid George and Job were nearly wrecked. Job changed his mind about the course a little too late and they had a narrow escape. They were whirled round and banged up against a cliff with the bottom of the canoe tipped to the rock and held there for a while, but fortunately did not turn over till an unusually tempestuous rush of water reached up and lifted the canoe from its perch down into the water again. Then tying a rope at either end they clambered out to a precarious perch on a slope in the cliff. By careful manoeuvring they succeeded in turning the canoe round and getting in again, thus escaping from the trap. Joe and Gilbert came through without mishap. Practically the whole river from Indian House Lake is like a toboggan slide. I shall be glad for everyone and especially for Job, when we have left the rapids behind. He says be feels better to-night. Saw fresh caribou tracks upon the terrace. Have been finding beautiful bunches of harebell (Cornua uniflora) in the clefts of the rocks along the river. They are very lovely. Once to-day the lonely cry of a wolf came down to us from high up on the mountain side. The mountains are splendid. We are in the midst of scenes which have a decidedly Norwegian look. Have passed one river and several good-sized streams coming in from the east and one of some size from west, but we have seen nothing from the west which could be called a river. Much more water comes in from the east.

"As we turned northward this evening just above camp a wind came up the valley, that felt as if straight from the Arctic. Fire in an open place to-night, and I do not like to go out to supper. It is so cold. Thinking now we may possibly get to the post day after to-morrow. George says be thinks the river must be pretty straight from here. I rather think it will take us a little more than two days. All feel that we may have good hope of catching the steamer. Perhaps we shall get to tide water to-morrow. There have been signs of porcupine along the way to-day, and one standing wigwam. There is a big bed of moss berries (a small black berry, which grows on a species of moss and is quite palatable) right at my tent door to-night. So strange, almost unbelievable, to think we are coming so near to Ungava. I begin to realise that I have never actually counted on being able to get there."

The country grew more and more mountainous and rugged and barren. The wood growth, which is of spruce and tamarack, with here and there a little balsam, was for some distance below the Barren Grounds Water rather more abundant than it had been along the lake shores. At best it was but a narrow belt along the water edge covering the hills to a height of perhaps two hundred feet and dwindling gradually toward the north, till in some places it was absent altogether and our tents were pitched where no trees grew. The ridges on either side crossed each other almost at right angles, turning the river now to the northeast, again to the northwest. Down the mountain sides, broad bands of white showed where the waters of numberless lakes and streams on the heights came tumbling down to join the river, or again a great gap in the solid mountain of rock let through a rush of blue-green, foaming water. The hills have the characteristic Cambrian outline and it is the opinion of Mr. Low that this formation extends continuously eastward from the Kaniapiscau to the George. The mountains on the right bank were more rugged and irregular than those on the left, and Bridgman Mountains in places stand out to the river quite distinct and separate, like giant forts. On the morning of August 24th they had closed round us as if to swallow us up, and gazing back from our lunching place George said, with something of awe in his tone, "It looks as if we had just got out of prison."

And still the river roared on down through its narrow valley, at Helen Falls dropping by wild and tempestuous cascades, and then by almost equally wild rapids, to a mile below where it shoots out into an expansion with such terrific force as to keep this great rush of water above the general level for some distance out into the lake. Here we made the longest portage of the journey down the George River, carrying the stuff one and a quarter mile.

Below Helen Falls the mountains spread in a wider sweep to the sea, and the river gradually increased in width as it neared Ungava. Still it flowed on in rapids. So often we had asked each other, "Will they never end?" However, in the afternoon on August 26th, we reached smooth water, and had a few hours' paddling. Then darkness began to close in. If only we could keep on! I knew from my observation that day we could not be many miles from our journey's end now; but it was not to be that we should reach our destination that night, and camp was pitched at a point, which I thought must be about seven or eight miles above the post.

It was very disappointing, and when George said, "If the ship is there they will be sure to try to get off Saturday night," I felt rather desperate. Still it would not do to take chances with the George River in the dark.

In spite of anxieties I slept that night but felt quite strung in the morning. At breakfast I used the last of the crystalose in my tea. It seemed very wonderful that the little ounce bottle of this precious sweet had lasted us as long as sixty pounds of sugar. There was just a little of our tea left, and I filled the bottle with it to keep as a souvenir of the trip. The remainder I put into one of the waterproof salt-shakers and this I gave to George. I learned later that there was a bit of quiet fun among the men as I did it. They had no great faith in my calculations, and it was their opinion that the tea would probably taste quite good at lunch.

After what seemed an unnecessarily long time, the camp things were again in the canoe and we were off. About a mile below the camp we found that the rapids were not yet passed. Here a heavy though short one made a portage necessary and then we dropped down to where the river spreads out to two miles or more in width. For several miles we paddled on in smooth water, the river swinging a little to the west. How eagerly I watched the point where it turned again to the north for beyond that we should see the post. As we neared the bend there was an exciting escape from running into an unsuspected rapid. Nothing was to be seen ahead but smooth water. The wind was from the south and not a sound was heard till, suddenly, we found ourselves almost upon the brink of the slope, and only by dint of hard paddling reached the shore just at its edge. It was the first and only time we had been caught in this way. Again came the question, "Will they never end?"

The rapids stretched on before us turbulent and noisy, as before, first west then swinging abruptly to the north. Joe and Gilbert decided to portage across the point, but George and Job after much consideration prepared to run down in the canoe while I walked across to the little bay below.

As they were starting off I said to George, "When you get out beyond those points you should be able to see the island opposite the post."

"All right, I'll watch for it," he replied with a smile, and they started.

Pushing off, they worked the canoe cautiously out to where they meant to take the rapid. It was something more of a feat then they had looked for, and suddenly after strenuous but ineffectual efforts to make the canoe do what they wanted, they dropped into the bottom, and to my amazement I saw it shoot forward stern foremost into the rapid. The men had been quick as the water though, and in dropping to their places had turned about, so that they were not quite helpless. I stood watching them, hardly daring to breathe.

The canoe danced like an autumn leaf in the swells of the rapid, and Job's excited shouting came faintly over the sound of the water. At what a pace they were going? Was the canoe under control? I could not tell. What would happen when they reached the point where the water swings round to the north again? In an agony of suspense I watched and waited. Now they were nearing the critical point. And—now—*they had passed it*, and with a wild cry of triumph turned towards the little bay below. As they drew in to where I waited for them, George waved his cap to me and shouted, "I saw the island."

We passed out beyond the point below and there it lay, some miles away, in the quiet water, with the sunshine of the calm Sabbath morning flooding down upon it. But the post was not yet in sight. Quite out of harmony with the still dignity of the day and the scenes of desolate grandeur about was the mind within me. The excitement at the rapid had seemed to increase the strain I was under, and every moment it became more intense. I did wish that the men would not chat and laugh in the unconcerned way they were doing, and they paddled as leisurely as if I were not in a hurry at all. If only I could reach the post and ask about the ship! If only I might fly out over the water without waiting for these leisurely paddles! And now, from being in an agony of fear for their lives, my strong desire was to take them by their collars and knock their heads together hard. This was not practicable in the canoe, however, and I was fain to control myself as best I might.

Once I said to George, "Do hurry a little," and for two minutes he paddled strenuously; but soon it was again the merry chat and the leisurely dip, dip of the paddles. I think they were laughing at me a little and had also in their minds the fun it would be to see me bring out my precious tea again for lunch.

Suddenly we descried a white speck on a point some distance away, and drawing nearer saw people moving about. Then we discovered that a boat was out at some nets, and on reaching it found an Eskimo fisherman and his son taking in the catch. He smiled broadly as he came to the end of his boat to shake hands with us, and my heart sank dully, for his face and manner plainly indicated that he had been expecting us. This could only be explained by the fact that the ship had been to the post bringing with her the news of my attempted crossing. We spoke to him in English, which he seemed to understand, but replied in Eskimo, which we were helpless to make anything of, and after a vain struggle for the much desired news as to the ship, we left him and proceeded on our way.

I sat thinking desperately of the Eskimo, of the way he had received us and its portent. There could be only one explanation. I had no heart now for the competition as to who should first sight the post. Yet how we hope even when there is nothing left to us but the absence of certainty! I could not quite give up yet. Suddenly George exclaimed, "There it is." Somehow he seemed nearly always to see things first.

There it was deep in a cove, on the right bank of the river, a little group of tiny buildings nestling in at the foot of a mountain of solid rock. It seemed almost microscopic in the midst of such surroundings. The tide was low and a great, boulder-strewn, mud flat stretched from side to side of the cove. Down from the hills to the east flowed a little stream winding its way through a tortuous channel as it passed out to the river. We turned into it and followed it up, passing between high mud-banks which obscured the post till we reached a bend where the channel bore away to the farther side of the cove. Then to my surprise the men suddenly changed paddles for poles and turning the bows inshore poled right on up over the mud-bank. It was such a funny and novel performance that it snapped the spell for me, and I joined with the men in their shouts of laughter over the antics of the canoe on the slippery mud-bank. When we finally reached the top and slid out on to the flat, we saw a man, who we supposed must be Mr. Ford, the agent at the post, coming over the mud with his retinue of Eskimo to meet us.

We were all on our feet now waiting. When he came within hearing, I asked if he were Mr. Ford, and told him who I was and how I had come there. Then came the, for me, great question, "Has the ship been here?"

He said, "Yes."

"And gone again?"

"Yes. That is—what ship do you mean? Is there any other ship expected here than the Company's ship?"

"No, it is the Company's ship I mean, the *Pelican*. Has she been here?"

"Yes," he said, "she was here last September. I expect her in September again, about the middle of the month or later."

CHAPTER XVIII

THE RECKONING

There are times when that which constitutes one's inner self seems to cease. So it was with me at the moment Mr. Ford uttered those last words. My heart should have swelled with emotion, but it did not. I cannot remember any time in my life when I had less feeling.

Mr. Ford was asking me to come with him to the post house, and looking at my feet. Then George was seen to rummage in one of the bags and out came my seal-skin boots which I had worn but once, mainly because the woman at Northwest River post who made them had paid me the undeserved compliment of making them too small. My "larigans," which had long ago ceased to have any waterproof qualities, were now exchanged for the seal-skins, and thus fortified I stepped out into the slippery mud. So with a paddle as staff in one hand and Mr. Ford supporting me by the other, I completed my journey to the post.

At the foot of the hill below the house, Mrs. Ford stood waiting. Her eyes shone like stars as she took my hand and said, "You are very welcome, Mrs. Hubbard. Yours is the first white woman's face I have seen for two years." We went on up the hill to the house. I do not remember what we talked about, I only remember Mrs. Ford's eyes, which were very blue and very beautiful now in her excitement. And when we reached the little piazza and I turned to look back, there were the men sitting quietly in the canoes. The Eskimo had drawn canoes, men and outfit across the mud to where a little stream slipped down over a gravelly bed, which offered firmer footing, and were now coming in single file towards the post each with a bag over his shoulder.

Why were the men sitting there? Why did they not come too?

Suddenly I realised that with our arrival at the post our positions were reversed. They were my charges now. They had completed their task and what a great thing they had done for me. They had brought me safely, triumphantly on my long journey, and not a hair of my head had been harmed. They had done it too with an innate courtesy and gentleness that was beautiful, and I had left them without a word. With a dull feeling of helplessness and limitation I thought of how differently another would have done. No matter how I tried, I could never be so generous and self-forgetful as he. In the hour of disappointment and loneliness, even in the hour of death, he had taken thought so generously for his companions. I, in the hour of my triumph, had forgotten mine. We were like Light and Darkness and with the light gone how deep was the darkness. Once I had thought I stood up beside him, but in what a school had I learned that I only reached to his feet. And now all my effort, though it might achieve that which he would be glad and proud of, could never bring him back.

I must go back to the men at once; and leaving Mr. and Mrs. Ford I slipped down the hill again, and out along the little stream across the cove. They came to meet me when they saw me coming and Heaven alone knows how inadequate were the words with which I tried to thank them. We came up the hill together now, and soon the tents were pitched out among the willows. As I watched them from the post window busy about their new camping ground, it was with a feeling of genuine loneliness that I realised that I should not again be one of the little party.

Later came the reckoning, which may be summed up as follows:—

Length of Journey:—576 miles from post to post (with 30 miles additional to Ungava Bay covered later in the post yacht Lily).

Time:—June 27th to August 27th. Forty-three days of actual travelling, eighteen days in camp.

Provisions:—750 lbs. to begin with, 392 lbs. of which was flour. Surplus, including gifts to Nascaupee Indians, 150 lbs., 105 lbs. of which was flour, making the average amount consumed by each member of the party, 57 1/2 lbs.

Results:—The pioneer maps of the Nascaupee and George Rivers, that of the Nascaupee showing Seal Lake and Lake Michikamau to be in the same drainage basin and which geographers had supposed were two distinct rivers, the Northwest and the Nascaupee, to be one and the same, the outlet of Lake Michikamau carrying its waters through Seal Lake and thence to Lake Melville; with some notes by the way on the topography, geology, flora and fauna of the country traversed.

It is not generally borne in mind by those who have been interested in Mr. Hubbard and his last venture, that he did not plan his outfit for the trip which they made. The failure to find the open waterway to Lake Michikamau, which has already been discussed, made the journey almost one long portage to the great lake. But even so, if the season of unprecedented severity in which my husband made his journey, could have been exchanged for the more normal one in which I made mine, he would still have returned safe and triumphant, when there would have been only praises for his courage, fortitude and skill in overcoming the difficulties which lie across the way of those who would search out the hidden and untrod ways.

Nevertheless rising far above either praise or blame stands the beauty of that message which came out from the lonely tent in the wilderness. In utter physical weakness, utter loneliness, in the face of defeat and death, my husband wrote that last record of his life, so triumphantly characteristic, which turned his defeat to a victory immeasurably higher and more beautiful than the success of his exploring venture could ever have been accounted, and thus was compassed the higher purpose of his life.

For that it had been given to me to fulfill one of those lesser purposes by which he planned to build up a whole, that would give him the right to stand among those who had done great things worthily, I was deeply grateful. The work was but imperfectly done, yet I did what I could.

The hills were white with snow when the ship came to Ungava. She had run on a reef in leaving Cartwright, her first port of call on the Labrador coast; her keel was ripped out from stem to stern, and for a month she had lain in dry dock for repairs at St. John's, Newfoundland. It was October 22nd when I said good-bye to my kind friends at the post and in ten days the *Pelican* landed us safe at Rigolette. Here I had the good fortune to be picked up by a steamer bound for Quebec; but the wintry weather was upon us and the voyage dragged itself out to three times its natural length, so that it was the evening of November 20th, just as the sun sank behind the city, that the little steamer was docked at Quebec, and I stepped from her decks to set foot once again in "God's country."

DIARY OF LEONIDAS HUBBARD, JR. KEPT DURING HIS EXPEDITION INTO LABRADOR

Tuesday, July 7th—Last night moonlight and starry and fine. This morning the shore of Labrador spread out before us in the sunshine. It calls ever so hard, and I am hungry to tackle it. Landed this A.M. at Indian Harbour. George and I went ashore in the canoe; Wallace in ship's boat. Lot of fishermen greeted us. Find all men and women on the coast are Newfoundland men, and "Liveyeres" (Live-heres). The former come up to fish in summer and are the aristocrats. The latter are the under-crust. Could not get any one to take us to Rigolette. Spent the afternoon getting outfit together—assorting and packing—weighing it and trying it in the canoe, while line of Newfoundland salts looked on, commented, and asked good-natured questions. Canoe 18 feet, guide's special, Oldtown, canvas. Weight about 80. Tent—miner's tent, pole in front, balloon silk, weight 6 lbs., dimensions 6 1/2 x 7. Three pairs 3-lb. blankets; two tarpaulins about 6 x 7; three pack straps; two 9-inch duck waterproof bags, hold 40 lbs. each; three 12-inch bags; 3 1/4 x 4 1/4 kodak; 30 rolls films, one dozen exposures each, in tin cases with electrician's tape water-proofing; one dozen small waterproof bags of balloon silk, for sugar, chocolate, note-books and sundries. Wallace and I each have one extra light weight 45-70 rifle, smokeless powder. Also one pistol each, diamond model, 10-inch barrel, for partridges. For grub we have four 45-lb. sacks of flour; 30 lbs. bacon; 20 lbs. lard; 30 lbs. sugar; 14 lbs. salt; 3 or 4 lbs. dried apples from home; 10 lbs. rice; 20 lbs. erbswurst; 10 lbs. pea flour in tins; 10 lbs. tea; 5 lbs. coffee; 6 chocolate; 10 hardtack; 10 lbs. dried milk. Put all in canoe, got in ourselves, and found we could carry it O.K.

Wednesday, July 8th.—Took observation at noon. Lat. 54 degrees 28 minutes. Steve Newell, a liveyere from Winter's Cove, offered to take us to Rigolette for fifteen dollars. "Would I give him $1 to get a bit of grub for his family?" Got flour and molasses. Started in the *Mayflower*, a leaky little craft, about 5 P.M. No wind to speak of. Cold drizzle and fog. About 11 we landed at Winter's Cove. Nasty place to land among the rocks on a desolate point. From a shanty on the beach came a yelling and hallooing from several voices to know who we were and what we were doing. Went into cabin, two rooms—one frame and the other sod. Room about 12 x 14—desolate. Two women like furies—ragged, haggard, brown, hair streaming. One had baby in her arms; two small girls and a boy. One of women Steve's mother. Dirty place, but better than the chilling fog. Glad to get in. Fire started. Stove smoked till room was full. Little old lamp, no chimney. We made coffee and gave coffee and hard-tack to all. Women went into other room with children. We spread tarpaulin and blankets, and lay on floor; so did Steve. Women talked loudly.

Thursday, July 9th.—Started at 5 A.M., launching boat after Steve had said, "Don't know as we can launch 'er, sir." Fog. Offered Steve chart and compass. "Ain't got no learnin', sir. I can't read." So I directed course in fog and Steve steered. Later, clear, fair, high wind. Steve cool, nervy, tireless. He traps foxes and shoots partridges in winter. Buys flour and molasses. Got too windy to travel. Landed at Big Black Island to wait for lower wind. George used up—lumbago. Put him to bed and put on mustard plaster. Bought salmon of Joe Lloyd. Lives in 10 x 12 shanty, hole in roof for smoke to escape. Eskimo wife. "Is all the world at peace, sir?" He came from England. Hungry for news. Had trout smoking in chimney. A little wood on this island, and moss, thick and soft. Wind high, and George sick, so did not go on. Gave George two blankets and tarpaulin. Did not pitch tent. Wallace and I threw tent down and lay on it. Pulled his blanket over us and slept. Still sunlight at 11. Whales snorting in the bay. Big gulls croaking.

Friday, July 10th.—Awoke at 1 A.M. Bright moonlight, made coffee and milk. Called men. George very bad. Portaged outfit 200 yards to boat. Found her high. Worked till 4.30 to launch her. Little wind. Made Pompey Island at 11. Saw many whales and seals. Caught caplin on fish-hook tied to stick jerking them. Stopped on Pompey for lunch. Mossy island of Laurentian rock. Saw steamer in distance. Put off—fired three or four shots. Got only a salute. Put off in canoe to head her off. She came about. Was the *Virginia Lake*. Took us on board and brought us to Rigolette. Mr. Frazer, H.B.C. Agent here, to whom I had letter from Commissioner Chippman of the H.B. Co., took us in, as the Company's men always do. Made us at home. Seems fine to be on land again at a Company post. George better. Eskimo dogs. Eskimo men and women, breeds lumbermen, trappers, fishermen, two clerks. All kindly—even the dogs. All talkative and hungry for outside visitors.

Saturday, July 11th.—Awoke from bad dream of trouble getting somewhere to realise that I was at a post. Mighty good awakening. George better. Trying to get data as to Northwest River. No Indians here. White men and Eskimo know little about it. Capt. Joe Blake says Grand Lake good paddling. Forty miles long. Nascaupee River empties into it. Says Red River comes into it about 15 miles above its mouth. His son Donald came from his traps on Seal Lake to-day. Says same. Has crossed it about 50 miles above its mouth in winter. Has heard from some one that Montagnais Indians say it comes from Michikamau. Does not know. Says it is shallow. This seems to be what Low has mapped as Northwest River. Donald says not much game on it. Others who have not been there, say plenty. All report bear. Man who lives on river just above Grand Lake in winter to trap, missing. Supposed drowned. Donald says a chance seal in Seal Lake. Has shot 'em but never killed one. Little game there to eat. May be fish. Does not know. Does not fish himself. Takes flour, pork, tea and "risin." Porcupines. We can live on them. Hard to get definite data; but that makes the work bigger.

Sunday, July 12th.—Birthday. "Bruise" for breakfast. Hard-tack, fish, pork, boiled together—good. "Two more early risin's, and then duff and bruise," is said to be a Thursday remark of the fishermen. The *Pelican* came in to-day. Stole in in fog, and whistled before flag was up. Good joke on Post. Big day. *Pelican* goes from here to York, stopping at Ungava on way out and comes back again. Brings supplies. Captain Gray came on shore. Has been with company thirty years, in northern waters fifty years. Jolly, cranky, old fellow. "You'll never get back" he says to us. "If you are at Ungava when I get there I'll bring you back." Calder, lumberman on Grand River and Sandwich Bay, here says we can't do it. Big Salmon stuffed and baked for dinner—bully. George says he is ready to start now. Prophecies that we can't do it, don't worry me. Have heard them before. Can do it. WILL.

Monday, July 13th.—This noon the *Julia Sheridan*, Deep Sea Mission Boat, Dr. Simpson, came. We said good-bye and embarked for Northwest River. Had good informal supper in little cabin. Good easy yachting time. Stopped about 11 P.M. behind St. John's Island for the night.

Tuesday, July 14th.—Landed about 2 P.M. at Northwest River. Thomas M'Kenzie in charge. Bully fellow, all alone, lonesome, but does not admit it. Tall, wiry, hospitable in the extreme. Not busy in winter. Traps some. Wishes he could go with us. Would pack up to-night and be ready in the morning. Can get no definite information as to our route. M'Kenzie says we are all right; can make it of course. Gave away bag of flour. Discarded single blanket, 5 lbs. can lard. Got at Rigolette yesterday, 10 lbs. sugar, 5 lbs. dried apples, 4 1/2 lbs. tobacco. Bought here 5 lbs. sugar. M'Kenzie gave me an 8 lb. 3 in. gill net.

Wednesday, July 15th.—Wind light, southeast all day, light clouds. Lat. noon 53 degrees 35 minutes. Left Northwest River Post 9 A.M. Camped early because of rain and stream which promised trout. No trout caught. Lake looks like Lake George, with lower hills. Much iron ore crops from bluffs on south side. Makes me a bit homesick to think of Lake George. Wish I could see my girl for a while and be back here. Would like to drop in at the Michigan farm too.

Thursday, July 16th.—Fair day. Wind southeast. Lat. at noon 53 degrees 45 minutes. Six miles above Grand Lake on Northwest River. Started at 5.30 A.M. At 9 rounded point and saw mouth of river. George and I ferried outfit across northwest arm of lake in two loads. Wind too high for whole load. Saw steel trap. Probably belonged to poor M'Lean, who was drowned. Had cup of tea at 10. Stopped at noon three-quarters of an hour for observation. Northwest River runs through spruce-covered valley, between high hills, easily seen from lake, but not in river as spruce is too close. In many places high banks, many turns, many little rapids. Water low. Have to pole and track. See that we have our work cut out. Doubt if we can make more than 10 miles a day up this river. I took tracking line; George and Wallace the poles. Sand flies awful—nasty, vindictive, bite out chunks, and streak our hands and faces with blood. Mosquitoes positively friendly by contrast. Tried net. Could not see, then tried dope—some help. Eating much and not rustling for fish or game. Want to lighten outfit.

Friday, July 17th.—Rain and clouds. Rained hard in the night. Awoke dreading to start out in it. Got breakfast to let George sleep. Water so shoal and swift that we would take part of outfit and return for the rest. Most places had to track, I pulling on rope while Wallace and George waded, and pushed and dragged the canoe.

Saturday, July 18th.—Bright, clear day. Lat. 53 degrees 45 minutes 30 seconds. Started out with full load and kept it most of the day. Had to portage half load a few times. Awful work all day. Rapids continuously. I waded with line while George and Wallace dragged and lifted. All enjoyed the forenoon's work, and no one depressed when P.M. weariness began. No game. Bear and some caribou tracks. Have not seen a partridge or porcupine. Seem to be few fish. They come later and farther on.

Sunday, July 19th.—Minimum temp. last night 38 degrees. Fine day and warm. Stayed in camp all day to rest. I got up at 7 and caught about twenty trout, small. All pretty tired and enjoyed the long sleep. At noon George and I started up the river, following the hills. Found small rocky stream coming in about 1 mile up. Suppose it is the Red Wine River. Two miles up a 2-mile stretch of good water. Best of all the portage route leading in at the foot. We followed this over the hill to the Red Wine River, and found old cuttings. This pleases us a heap. It shows that we are on the old Montagnais trail, that we will probably have their portage routes clear through, and that they probably found lakes and good water farther up, or they would never have fought this bad water. To-morrow we will tackle the 2-mile portage with light hearts. We are 3 miles south of where Low's map places us. Am beginning to suspect that the Nascaupee River, which flows through Seal Lake, also comes out of Michikamau, and that Low's map is wrong. Bully stunt if it works out that way. Saw lots of caribou and fresh bear tracks. Trout went fine for supper. Flies very bad. Our wrists burn all the time.

Monday, July 20th.—Minimum temp. last night 37 degrees. Bright day. Flies awful. I got breakfast while George cut portage through swamp, and then we groaned all day—through the swamp 1 1/2 miles—across two streams, up steep hill, then along old trail to foot of smooth water above these rapids. Covered route mainly three times. All very tired. George worked like a hero.

Tuesday, July 21st.—Minimum temp. 36 degrees. Trapped bad three-quarter mile. George and I scouted ahead 6 miles. Climbed hills 600 feet high. Caribou and bear tracks. Crossed two or three creeks. Found old trail and wigwam poles and wood. George says winter camp from size of wood; can't follow it. Tracked quarter mile more, and started on long portage. Went half mile and camped. Flies bad; gets cold after dark, then no flies. Stars, fir tops, crisp air, camp fire, sound of river, hopeful hearts. Nasty hard work, but this pays for it.

Wednesday, July 22nd.—Minimum temp. 33 degrees, 60 degrees in tent at 6 A.M. Torture. All work to cross 2 1/2 mile portage. Sun awful. Flies hellish. All too tired to eat at noon. Cold tea and cold erbswurst. Cached 80 rounds 45-70 cartridges, 300-22s. too heavy. Too tired at last to mind flies. Rested hour under tent front, all of us. Diarrhoea got me—too much water drinking yesterday I guess. Shot partridge, first seen on trip. Jumped up on log before me, waited for me to drop pack and load pistol. Camp on partridge point. Bird seasoned a pot of erbswurst. Dreamed about home as I worked and rested.

Thursday, July 23rd.—George and Wallace scouted for trails and lakes. I lay in tent, diarrhoea. Took Sun Cholera Mixture. Tore leaves from Low's book and cover from this diary. These and similar economies lightened my bag about 5 lbs. New idea dawned on me as I lay here map gazing. Portage route leaves this river and runs into southeast arm of Michikamau. Will see how guess turns out. Heat in tent awful—at noon 104 degrees; out of tent at 1 P.M. 92 degrees. Diarrhoea continued all day. No food but tea and a bit of hard-tack. George back about 7.30. Wallace not back. Not worried. Has probably gone a little too far and will stay out. Has tin cup and erbswurst. George reports branching of river and a good stretch of calm water.

Friday, July 24th.—George produced yellowlegs shot yesterday. He carried pack up river 2 miles. Diarrhoea. In tent I studied how to take time with sextant. Observation failed. Much worried over Wallace till he came in about 7 P.M. Compass went wrong; he lay out overnight. Stewed yellowlegs and pea meal to-night.

Saturday, July 25th.—Four miles. Weak from diarrhoea. Portaged one load each 4 miles south side of stream to open water. Back to camp. I took another load; George and Wallace followed, trying to drag canoe up river. I made camp. They came in after dark, tired out. Canoe left 2 miles down stream. Wallace shot partridge with pistol. Came near going over falls with pack round his neck. Drizzled all day. Heavy rain to-night. Great relief from heat. Flies very bad in afternoon and evening.

Sunday, July 26th.—Rain most of the clay. Lay in tent in A.M. hoping to be better of diarrhoea. Read Low's report, *etc.* Trouble better.

Monday, July 27th.—Spent A.M. and two hours P.M. bringing up canoe, dragging half way, George carrying rest. Started on at 4. Alternate pools and rapids. Rapids not bad—go up by dragging and tracking. After 1 1/2 mile camped.

Tuesday, July 28th.—Temp. 6 A.M. 46 degrees. Three miles. Cool, cloudy, spell of sunshine now and then. Cold, nasty wading all A.M. to make a mile. Fine portaging in P.M., just cool enough, no flies. Pretty nearly blue in A.M. over lack of progress. Two miles in P.M. brightened things up. By fire between logs we dry, clothes now in evening. All tired out. Low new moon.

Wednesday, July 29th.—Temp. 6 A.M. 58 degrees. Worked 4 miles. Small ponds alternating with rapids. Portage 1 mile in P.M. Very tired. Tea, and finished fine.

Thursday, July 30th.—Temp. 6 A.M. 39 degrees. Paddled through a succession of ponds about a quarter of a mile long each, tracking or dragging over little falls or rapids between. Made portage of 100 rods in P.M. Need fish now. Grub not so heavy as it was. Were starting to dry blankets at fire when rain started. All crawled into tent. Need rain to raise river. Plenty caribou signs—two old wigwams (winter) on rock. No fish but 6-7 inch trout. Bully camp to-night.

Friday, July 31st.—Temp. 6 A.M. 56 degrees. Rain all day. Two rivers puzzled us. Came together just above our camp. One comes over a fall from the south side;

other rough, comes from northwest. South branch comes from west, better, more level. Little ponds between falls and short rapids. Scouted. Think south branch Low's Northwest River. Wallace caught bully mess of trout while George and I were scouting. George found old wigwam about a quarter of a mile up south branch; also a winter blaze crossing stream north to south, fresh. Trappers' line, think. Blake or M'Lean. Wigwam old. Rain bad. River not very good, some ponds, some portage, some dragging. Up south branch three-quarters of a mile stopped for lunch. Stopped after a quarter of a mile portage for a scout. Wallace and I made camp in rain while George scouted. George reports 1 1/2 mile bad river,, then level, deep ponds, very good. Caught trout. Rainy camp.

Saturday, August 1st.—Rained steadily all night and to-day. Tired, chilled, ragged. Wallace not well and things damp. Stayed in camp all day. Hoped to dry things out. Too much rain. Went out in bare feet and drawers and caught ten trout.

Sunday, August 2nd.—Cleared this A.M. Boys dried camp while I caught twenty-four trout, some half pounders. Getting bigger, nearer Height of Land we hope reason. Water higher. Will help us. Two cans baking powder spoiled. Good feed of trout. Not a bit tired of trout yet. Observation shows 53 degrees 46 minutes 12 seconds lat. Went 3 miles in P.M. and camped.

Monday, August 3rd.—Temp. 6 A.M. 56 degrees. Big day. At foot of a portage as we were getting ready to pack, I saw four wild geese coming down stream. Grabbed rifle, four cartridges in it. George got Wallace's rifle. All dropped waiting for them to come round bend, 30 ft. away. George and I shot at once, both hitting leader. All started flapping along on top of water, up stream. I emptied my rifle on them, going at 40 to 50 yards, killing two more. Drew pistol and ran up and into stream and shot fourth in neck. Got all and threw fits of joy. Need 'em just now badly for grub. Through little lake beginning at head of water, quarter of a mile above, into meadow, fresh beaver house. At foot of rapid water, below junction of two streams, ate lunch. Trout half to three-quarter pounds making water boil. Caught several. From this point to where river branches to two creeks, we scouted. Think found old Montagnais portage. To-night heap big feed. George built fire as for bread-baking.

Tuesday, August 4th.—Temp. 6 A.M. 56 degrees. Portaged 1 mile to Montagnais Lake. Portage ran through bogs and over low ridges. I sat on edge of lake looking at rod, when a caribou waded into lake, not 100 feet away. Rifle at other end of portage. Hoped to find inlet to lake, but only one ends in bog. Lots of old cuttings at northwest corner of lake; two old wigwams. Troubled to know where to go from here. All scouted whole afternoon. Lake 1 mile west. Old trail runs towards it. George thinks caribou trail, no cuttings found on it yet. I think portage. Looks like portage we have followed and runs in right direction.

Wednesday, August 5th.—Portaged from camp on Montagnais Lake, 1 mile west to another lake. No signs of Indians here. Camped at west end of this. Saw two caribou. Dropped pack and grabbed rifle; was waiting for them 250 yards away when a cussed little long-legged bird scared them. At point near camp where lakes meet, I cast a fly, and half pound and pound fontanalis, as fast as I could pull them out. What a feed at 2 P.M. lunch. Climbing ridge, saw that lake empties by little strait into another small lake just alongside, at south. Stream flows from that south. Therefore we are on Hamilton River waters. George and I went scouting to bluffs we saw from trees on ridge. Both lost. George got back before dark. I spent night on hill, 2 miles southwest. No matches or grub. Scared a little. Heard big river, found it flows southeast. Must go into Hamilton, but it is a big one, several times as big as the Northwest at its biggest. Where does it come from? Can it be Michikamau?

Thursday, August 6th.—Slept some last night, lying on two dead spruce tops, too wet and cold to sleep very well. Mosquitoes awful. George went to my river. Wallace and I took canoe and went into lake north of here. Cuttings, winter. George found river to be big and deep. Straight, as though from Michikamau. Don't believe this little creek of a Northwest comes from there. Will portage to this river and try it.

Friday, August 7th.—Portaged 2 miles to river on our south; good paddling save for a rapid now and then. So big we think, Low's map to the contrary, that it comes from Michikamau. Anyway it comes from that way and will carry us a piece toward the big lake. No cuttings. Big trout despite east wind. Caught about fifteen. Cold wind drove away flies. Fire between big rocks. Moon over bluffs beyond. Fine evening. Fine river. Fine world. Life worth living.

Saturday, August 8th.—Nasty, cold, east wind. Went 4 1/2 miles through it all in good river with six short portages first three-quarter mile, and stopped about 1 P.M. to make Sunday camp and get fish. Put out net, ate our dried fish and by hard labour got a few more for supper. Only a bit of bread a day now, no grease, save a little bacon. All hungry for flour and meat.

Sunday, August 9th.—Raining this morning and most of the P.M. Cold, east wind. Caught about forty-five trout by hard effort, several 3/4 lb. each. George made paddle and scouted. Burned his knife.

Monday, August 10th.—Rain and east wind. Caught one big fish before breakfast. Wallace ate it. George and I ate pea meal. On first portage found old summer cuttings and wigwam poles. Feel sure that this was the old Montagnais route. Went 3 miles and crossed four portages. Then on strength of being on right road and needing fish, camped before noon. Mother's birthday. Ate some of her dried apples last night with sugar.

Tuesday, August 11th.—East wind. Warmer a little. Just a little rain. No fish biting. Slept late. Climbed ridge and tree. See ridge of high half barren hills away ahead. Think this the ridge east of Michikamau. Hungry all the time. Down to 40 lbs. of flour, 8 lbs. tea, about 20 lbs. pea meal, a bit of sugar, bacon, baking powder and dried apple, just a bit of rice. Saw mountains ahead from a bluff just below our evening camp. River runs north apparently; it must therefore be Low's Northwest River I think. Mountains look high and rugged, 10 to 25 miles away. Ought to get

113

good view of country from there, and get caribou and bear. Moccasins all rotten and full of holes. Need caribou. Need bear for grease. All hungry all day. George weak, Wallace ravenous; lean, gaunt and a bit weak myself. Fish braced us wonderfully.

Wednesday, August 12th.—Best day of trip. Started late. Cloudy, damp. I took pack over half mile portage and stopped to fish. Fourteen trout. Three portages and then—glory! Open water. Five miles and stopped for lunch, with good water before and behind for first time since Grand Lake. Old wigwam and broken-down canoe at lunch place. Ate trout and loaf of bread. Hungry. Started again, hoping for stream to fish in. Made 3 miles. Then a big bull caribou splashed into the water of a bayou 200 yards ahead. Wallace in bow took shot, high and to the left. I raised sights to limit and held high. Did not think of sport, but grub, and was therefore cool. As first shot George said, "Good, you hit him." He started to sink, but walked up a bank very slowly. I shot two more times, Wallace once and missed. George and I landed and started towards spot. Found caribou down, trying to rise. Shot him in breast, cut throat. George made stage for drying. Wallace and I dressed caribou. Wallace put up tent. I started meat from bones in good strips to dry. Then all sat down and roasted steaks on sticks, and drank coffee, and were supremely happy. We will get enough dried meat to give us a good stock.

Thursday, August 13th.—Worked at getting caribou skin tanned in A.M. Ate steak for breakfast, liver for dinner, ribs for supper. No bread, just meat. Wallace and I started in canoe to look for fish and explore a bit. Found rapid 2 miles above. Very short, good portage, old wigwam, good water ahead. Too cold to fish. Cloudy day, but got blankets aired and dried. River seems to run to northeast of ridge of quite high mountains, 6 to 10 miles ahead. Very tired or lazy to-day. May be meat diet, may be relaxation from month of high tension. Think the latter. Mended pants. One leg torn clear down the front. Patched with piece of flour sack.

Friday, August 14th.—George and Wallace left in canoe with tin cups, tea and some caribou ribs, to scout river above and climb hills. I put some ashes and water on caribou skin. Just starting to shed. Studied map and Low's book. Wish we could descend this river on way out and map it.

Saturday, August 15th.—Cloudy again this morning. Sprinkle or two. Wallace and George not back. Wallace and George came at dusk; tired out and none too hopeful. Found stream coming from a little lake with two inlets. Followed one west to mountains; it turned to a brook, ended in mountains. Other went so much east they fear it ends in lakes there. Think maybe they lost the river. Hungry as bears. Stayed out to explore this east branch. The three days' inaction and their story of doubtful river, depressed me. If the way to Michikamau is still so doubtful, after more than four weeks of back-breaking work, when will we get there, and when to the caribou grounds, and when home? I'd like to be home to-night and see my girl and the people, and eat some bread and real sweet coffee or tea or chocolate. How hungry I am for bread and sweets!

Sunday, August 16th.—Wind has changed at last to north. Not much of it. Clear and bright in early morning. Clouded at noon, so I am not sure my observation was just right, close to it though I think. 53 degrees 46 minutes 30 seconds. Have been coming nearly west, an angle to south and another to north. Last observation possible was two weeks ago to-day. Feel fine to-day. Good rest and good weather and grub are bully. Figure that east branch the boys saw must be Low's Northwest River, and must break through the mountains somewhere a little north. Anyway it can't run much east and must take us north and west through lake expansions close to the mountains. Then if it ends, it's up to us to portage over to the lake expansions Low sees on his Northwest River flowing out of Michikamau. Scraped flesh from caribou skin.

Monday, August 17th.—Temp. at 4.30 A.M. 29 degrees. Temp. noon 59 degrees. Ice on cups. First of season. Beautiful, clear day, north wind, slight. Flies bad in P.M. Went west of north 3 miles, following river to where it began to expand into lakes. Noon observation 53 degrees 43 minutes 19 seconds. Yesterday's observation wrong I think. In A.M. fished few minutes at foot of short rapids. About forty trout, one 16 inches long, biggest yet. Caught most on fins. Ate all for noon lunch, stopping at sand-beach on shore of very pretty little lake expansion. Had coffee too. In P.M. we turned west into some long narrow lakes, that extend into mountains, and have a current coming out. George and Wallace think from a previous look, that here is a portage trail to Michikamau's southeast bay. George explored while I worked at skin. George returned. No good so far as he saw, to cross here, but he did not do the thing thoroughly. However, I'll let it drop, for I believe the river goes east and north, and then west and breaks through mountains to Michikamau. Worried some. Time short and way not clear, but we'll get there if we have to take the canoe apart and walk across. May have to stay late on the George, and have to snowshoe to Northwest River and then across; but if it comes to that we'll do it. This snowshoe to Northwest River and then across to the St. Lawrence, by Kenamon and St. Augustine Rivers, appeals to me. Lots of old wigwams about, summer and winter. Stove was used in one. I think Indians hunted here. Caribou tracks on barren mountains.

Tuesday, August 18th.—Temp. 28 degrees at 4 A.M. Clear sky in morning. Much worried last night and this morning, about way to Michikamau. Started early, ready to go at the job harder than ever. Lake expansions, rapids, no signs of Indians. Afraid this a bad stretch which Indians avoided. Stopped at 10 A.M. for tea. Caught fourteen big trout there, in few minutes. Then river opened into long narrow lakes, and the going was bully. It turned west, or we did (it came from the west) and went into the mountains, and we fairly shouted for joy. George saw caribou. Turned out to be geese. Chased ahead them on bank. Shot old goose as she lay low in water, swimming and hiding. Broke old one's wing and took off leg. Then missed four shots. Gander took to woods. George took after young and killed one with pistol. Came and helped get wounded goose. Great chase. Trout, pounders, jumping like greedy hogs to fly. Took about fifty while boys were making two short portages in P.M. Bread, small loaf, coffee, sugar, goose, trout for supper. Big feed in celebration geese and good water. At end of to-day's course turned to right into wrong channel, into little narrow lake half mile long, prettiest I ever saw. Big barren

115

bluff rises from water on north, barren mountains a few miles to west, ridge of green to west, sun setting in faces to contrast and darken, two loons laughing, two otters swimming in lake. One seemed afraid and dived; other more bold, looked at us. Hoped to kill it to settle question of species, but did not get near enough. Good water ahead. Hope we are on the road to Michikamau.

Wednesday, August 19th.—Noon 53 degrees 50 minutes. Bright, clear in A.M. Southeast wind brought clouds. Began to rain as we went to bed. Spent whole day river hunting, paddling from arm to arm of the lakes. George and I climbed high barren ridge. Red berries and a few blue berries. Flock ptarmigan, rockers. I shot three with pistol, old one, two young, but could fly. Saw more mountains on all sides. Many lakes to east. Failure to find river very depressing to us all. Seems to end in this chain of lakes. Will retrace our way to last rapid to be sure, and failing to find stream, will start west up a creek valley on a long portage to Michikamau. Boys ready for it. I fear it will make us late, but see no other way. Glad Wallace and George are game. A quitter in the crowd would be fierce.

Thursday, August 20th.—Rain last night. Cloudy in A.M. Rain P.M. and night. Wind south. Stopped to mend moccasins and give caribou a bit more drying before we start to cross mountains. Looked ahead and saw two more lakes. May be a good deal of lake to help us. Mended moccasins with raw caribou skin. While George got lunch I took sixteen trout, fin for bait. In P.M. Wallace and I took canoe and went back over course to last rapid, exploring to see that we had not missed river. Sure now we have not. So it's cross mountains or bust, Michikamau or BUST. Wallace and I came upon two old loons and two young. Old tried to call us from young. Latter dived like fish. Caught one. Let it go again. We caught eighty-one trout at last rapid in about an hour, mostly half-pounders; fifteen about pounders, hung to smoke. Big feed for supper. Rest for to-morrow. Rained good deal. Sat under drying stage with a little fire, tarpaulin over us and had big supper—fried trout, trout roe, loaf of bread, coffee. Last of coffee. Hate to see it go. Little sugar left. A bit in morning and evening cups.

Friday, August 21st.—Rain all day. Wind changed to north, colder. Portaged to little lake above camp. Found wigwams at each end of portage. Looks like old Montagnais trail. Then more lakes and short portages. Made 4 miles very easily, then, after pot of tea and big trout feed, portaged 1 mile west to another little lake, just over Height of Land. Our stream tumbles off the mountain, and does not come from this last-named lake at all. Little 4-foot ridge turns it. Went into camp very early, chilled through.

Saturday, August 22nd.—Portaged across Height of Land. Delighted to find on end of lake to westward many Indian signs. Believe this enters southeast bay of Michikamau, or a lake connected with it. Rained hard by spells. West wind. Camped on island early in P.M. after a very short march, to repair canoe, and to wait for head wind to fall. Caribou meat roasted at noon. Two loaves of bread, dried apples and tea—no meat or fish—supper.

116

Sunday, August 23rd.—West wind. Rain and clear by spells. Drank last of chocolate—two pots—for breakfast. Dried blankets in a sunny spell, and about 10 A.M. started. Coming to point round which we expected to get view of lake ahead— "Like going into a room where there is a Christmas tree," said George. Narrow channel around point 2 1/2 miles from east end. Thence we saw a long stretch of lake running west. Believe it Michikamau's S.E. bay sure. Mighty glad. Ate boiled dried caribou, pea soup, tea. Dried caribou hurts our teeth badly. Went west 2 1/2 miles and climbed barren hill on north side of lake. Ate blue berries, bake-apple berries, and moss berries. Saw on north, water in big and little masses, also on N.W. many islands of drift, rocky and spruce clad. One long stretch of lake, like a river, runs east and west, about 2 miles north. Wonder if it is Low's Northwest River. Went west on our lake 3 miles. Caught a fish like pike, with big square head, 3 1/2 lbs. Found our lake ends, stream falling in from another lake west. Came back 2 miles to outlet into waters north. Camped. All feel bully. On Michikamau waters sure.

Monday, August 24th.—Rain, north wind, cold. In camp all day. Bad head wind. George and I scouted. All restless at inactivity but George. He calm, philosophical, cheerful, and hopeful always— a wonderful man.

Tuesday, August 25th.—Cold N.E. wind. Rain. Made start. Nasty portage into Northwest River (?). Wallace turned round and started to carry his pack back. Wind fair part of time. Part of time dangerously heavy. Landed on point running out from north shore. Wigwam poles. Have diarrhoea. All chilled. Not sure of way ahead, but not worried. Camped at 5 P.M. Nice camp in clump of balsam. Not craving bread so much. Idleness and a chance to think make us hungrier. Flies about gone. Proverb—On a wet day build a big fire.

Wednesday, August 26th.—Temp. at 5 A.M. 40 degrees. Bright and clear save for one shower in P.M. Started happy. Shot goose with pistol after long chase. Goose would dive repeatedly. Shot several times at rather long range. Paddled 20 to 25 miles on big lake running east and west. No outlet west. Came back blue and discouraged. Passed our camp of last night to climb a mountain on N.E. side. Caught very pretty 2-lb. pike trolling. Wallace and I got supper. George went to climb mountain, found river this side (west) of mountain, running into this lake from N.W. What is it? Low's Northwest River? Can't see what else. Glad again. Very hopeful. Sick and very weak. Diarrhoea. Pea meal and venison and goose liquor. Better. Bright northern lights.

Thursday, August 27th.—Bright and lightly clouded by spells. No rain. Northwest River panned out only a little stream. N.G. Guess we must portage. Desperate. Late in season and no way to Michikamau. One more try for inlet, and then a long nasty portage for the big lake. See little hope now of getting out before winter. Must live off country and take big chances. Camping near where we camped last night. Going up Northwest River and hunting outlets some more, took our time. Ran across geese this A.M. I went ashore and George and Wallace chased them close by. Shot leader with rifle. Then two young ones head close in shore. I killed one with pistol and two others started to flop away on top of water. Missed one with pistol, and killed other. While exploring a bay to N.W., we landed to climb ridge. George found three partridges. I shot one, wounded another, pistol. Camped to-night cheerful but desperate. All firm for progress to Michikamau. All willing to try a return in winter. Discussed it to-night from all sides. Must get a good place for fish and caribou and then freeze up, make snowshoes and toboggans and moccasins and go. Late home and they will worry. Hungry for bread, pork and sugar. How I like to think at night of what I'll eat, when I get home and what a quiet, restful time I'll have. Flies bad by spells to-day.

Friday, August 28th.—Temp. 6 A.M. 56 degrees. Back to northwest end of lake where bay runs north. Portaged to small shoal lakes and camped on north side, ready to start in A.M. Fixed moccasins in preparation for long portage. Made observation of sun and moon to-night, hoping to get longitude. All very tired, but feel better now. No bread today. No sugar. Don't miss latter much, but hungry for bread. Good weather. Shower or two. Writing by camp fire.

Saturday, August 29th.—Temp. 6 A.M. 38 degrees. Am writing a starter here, before beginning our march north. Wallace and George at breakfast now. I'm not. Sick of goose and don't want it. Ate my third of a loaf of bread lumpy without grease and soggy, but like Huyler's bonbons to our hungry palates. Dreamed of being home last night, and hated to wake. Jumped up at first light, called boys and built fire, and put on kettles. We must be moving with more ginger. It is a nasty feeling to see the days slipping by and note the sun's lower declination, and still not know our way. Outlet hunting is hell on nerves, temper and equanimity. You paddle miles and miles, into bay after bay, bay after bay, with maybe no result till you are hopeless. Ugh! This is a great relief to be about to start north through the woods— fairly high ground to start with—on a hunt for Michikamau. Hope we will not have swamps. Lakes will probably stop us and make us bring up the canoe. Good evening and we are happy, despite fact that grub is short and we don't know our way and all that.

Sunday, August 30th.—Beautiful, clear Sunday, but no Sunday rest for us. I jumped up early, called George, and built fire. Started at 5.54 A.M., portaging from little lake to little lake, north and west, to where we know Michikamau must lie, somewhere. For two days we have heard geese flying. Thought our goose chases over, but to-day five walked down bank into water ahead of canoe on a small lake. Wounded two at one shot with rifle. Two old ones flew. Left wounded to chase third young one. Shot and killed it with pistol. Could not find wounded. Made 3 miles before dinner. Good. In P.M. about 1 1/4 miles more. Then reached range of semi-barren ridges, running east and west, and seeming to reach to barren mountains north. George and I climbed first ridge from a little lake, with blue green, ocean-coloured water. Heard stream ahead. Little river running through ponds. George went back for outfit and Wallace. These are trying days. We are not quite up to normal strength. I think too much routine of diet, lack grease, sugar and grain foods. The feeling of not knowing where we are or how to get out adds to our weakness, still we are all cheerful and hopeful and without fear. Glad all of us to be here. How we will appreciate home and grub when we get out. I crawl into blankets while the boys smoke their evening pipe. Then I think of M. and our home at Congers, and plan how she and I will go to Canada or Michigan or somewhere, for a two week's vacation when I get home. I wonder when that will be.

Monday, .August 31st.—Ice on cups this morning. Thermometer out of order. Lat. 53 degrees 57 minutes. I hate to see August end with us so far from the George River, or so perplexed as to the road. We are in camp now, on the stream we reached last night. I am writing and figuring in the early morning. The whole character of our country changes here. Ridges and hills extending into mountains on the north. Must know what lies there before we proceed. George will scout. Wallace and I will dry fish. While George was scouting, I lay in tent awhile, too weak to fish even. Fish not biting though. Oh, but I'll be happy to see Michikamau! George returned late. Climbed mountains to north. Reports fair line of travel to northwest, long lakes and tolerable portages. Will go that way, I think. Wallace got a few trout. George killed two partridges with my pistol.

Tuesday, September 1st.—West wind. Fair, warm. Very weak to-day. Our stuff so light now we can take all but canoe at one trip over portage. Have just crossed portage from lake by yesterday's camp, to other lakelet N.W. Boys gone back for canoe. I sit here and write. Very rough portaging here, all rocks and knolls. Little clear lakes between. Have to put canoe into water every 40 rods or so. Shot a plover with pistol to cook with George's partridges. Later. Made about 4 1/2 miles. Caught about thirty-five trout at edge of lake where stream empties.

Wednesday, September 2nd.—West wind. Fixed moccasins in A.M. and started portage west. Camped in swamp.

Thursday, September 3rd.—Rain all day by spells. Wind west. Got up in rain, hating to leave blankets. At breakfast, bread and tea and venison. I took no tea. Am trying now just venison and fish broth. May agree with me better than tea. Don't miss sugar much any more, though I do plan little sweet feeds when I am out. Very nasty work in rain. Am well again and strong. Worked well. Portaged and paddled west 4 1/2 miles. Wallace turned round again and carried pack back to starting point. George and I carried canoe. Sky cleared in evening. Saw all day big spruce trees. Country here not burned I think.

Friday, September 4th.—Rain. West wind, Portaged west 1 1/2 miles, with two little lakes to help. Rain all time. Stopped to let George scout best way to big lake ahead. Thinks it is 3 miles away. Hope it leads to Michikamau. George and Wallace mending moccasins. George reports big water about 3 miles ahead. Hope Low's Northwest River lake expansions. Cannot be far now from Michikaman. Spent much time over map in P.M. Think we must start back 1st October to the St. Lawrence, if we can get guides. Otherwise to Northwest River and then snowshoe out.

Saturday, September 5th.—Rain by spells. West wind, cold. Awoke in rain. Last three nights have been as clear as crystal, beautiful moon. Then rain in the morning. Very disappointing. We waited a little while about getting up, hoping rain would stop. Slackened, and we started. Poor day's work. Portaged about 2 1/2 miles west. Came out on barrens and ate lot of blue berries. Saw big waters to west, big blue hill, blue sky-line where we hope Michikamau lies hidden. Pint berries raw for supper. Otherwise, venison and broth, thickened with three spoonfuls of flour, each meal.

Sunday, September 6th.—Temp. 5 A.M. 38 degrees. First snow came, mixed with nasty cold rain. Nasty, raw, west wind. Worked in it most of day, portaging 2 1/2 miles N.W. Tried carrying all stuff at one trip. Grub low. Big water ahead. Believe this big water will lead to Michikamau. Almost a desperate hope. If it does not and we find no water route, I scarcely see how we can reach the caribou grounds in time to see the crossing and meet the Nascaupees. Without that I am doubtful of the success of this trip, and failure makes me shudder. Besides it is liable to make us all very hungry. We must push on harder, that's all. And get there somehow.

Monday, September 7th.—Temp. at 5 A.M. 48 degrees. N.W. wind, slight. Rain by showers. On portage crossed worst swamp of trip. In to my knees and fell down with heavy pack on my back. Floundered out in nasty shape. Found small stream flowing N.W. toward our big water. I caught about thirty trout, not big, while Wallace and George brought up outfit and canoe by stream. Very slow work. All very hungry in P.M. Stopped for pot of soup. Found it getting dark and stopped to camp. Last meal of venison in bag. Must get fish. Ate half our trout to-night, boiled and thickened with flour. Drank last bit of cocoa. No sugar. Boys not scared. No talk of quitting. Don't just see where we are coming out.

Tuesday, September 8th.—Cold raw N.W. wind, no rain, partly clear. Observation noon, 54 degrees 1 minute 21 seconds. Aired and dried blankets. Followed stream down to very shoal bay of our big water, which like the will-o'-wisp has led us on. Only ten trout, mostly small. Weather too raw. Very depressing to have it so when meat is out. On to caribou grounds is the watchword. Gave up trouting and started west on our big lake. Stopped to climb mountain. Ate some cranberries. Saw a few old caribou tracks. Big mountain to west of us. Islands or something between, many low, flat, wooded.

Wednesday, September 9th.—BIG DAY. Warm, clear. Temp. 5 A.M. 29 degrees. Ice in cups. Slept without sweater or socks last night. Cold but slept well. Beautiful cold crisp morning. Up at first dawn. Inspiring, this good weather. George boiled a little bacon and rice together, and a little flour made sort of porridge for breakfast. Very, very good. No fish or game ahead. Went to big hill mentioned yesterday. George and I walked about 4 miles and back getting to its top through spruce burnings. Awful walking. Very tired when about to top. Wondering about next meal and thinness of soup mostly to blame, I guess. Then things began to get good. First we ran across a flock of ten ptarmigan. They were in the burned-over semi-barren of the hill-top. They seem to lack entirely the instinct to preserve themselves by flying. Only ran ahead, squatting in apparent terror every few feet. We followed with our pistols. I killed eight and George one, my last was the old bird, which for a time kept away from us, running harder than the rest, trying to hide among the Arctic shrubs. George says they are always tame on a calm day. Their wings are white, but the rest is summer's garb. "Not rockers, but the real kind," says George. Then we went on across the mountain top and looked west. *There was* MICHIKAMAU! And that's what made it a BIG DAY. A series of lake expansions runs east from it. We can see them among flat drift islands, cedar covered, and a ridge south, and a hill and the high lands north, and apparently a little river coming from the north, and pouring into the lake expansions some miles east of Michikamau. There is one main channel running east and south, in this expansion. It is north of the waters we are now in, and we can see no connection. However, there looks as if there might be one about 5 miles east of our big hill. Behind some barren ridges, about 50 feet high. So we are making for them to see what we can find. If no connection, we must portage, but we will not mind a little portage now, with Michikamau waters just over it. Westward from our hill are dozens of little lakes, and a good deal of low burned land. S.E. more lakes. Must be an easy portage from the lakes on which we were muddled two weeks ago. That's where we missed it, in not finding that portage.

Thursday, September 10th.—Wind west, cloudy. Temp. 5 A.M. 46 degrees. Rain in evening. Cut legs from old drawers and pulled them over pants as leggings. Went east looking for opening in N.W. River. Think we saw it in ridge to northeast, came S.W. Believe that we saw also opening into Michikamau's Bay which runs out of lake on S.E. side. Wind delayed, and we only got to foot of mountain from which we expect to see it. Camped. Rain commenced. While scouting I shot a large spruce partridge with pistol.

Friday, September 11th.—Raining in morning. Wind southwest. Temp. 49 degrees. Ate last meal of mother's sweet dried apples. We are on the verge of success apparently, in sight of Michikamau from which it is not far to the caribou grounds and the Nascaupees. Yet we are sick at heart at this long delay and the season's lateness and our barefoot condition. Yet no one hints at turning back. We could do so, and catch fish and eat our meal, for we know the way to within easy walking distance of Grand Lake, but the boys are game. If we only had a fish net we would be 0.K. My plan is to get a few fish if possible, push on at once to Michikamau somehow. Get to the George River, and find the Nascaupees. Then if the caribou migration is not over, we will kill some of the animals, dry them up and get as far back as possible before freezing up and leaving the canoe. Then, unless we can get some one to show us to the St. Lawrence, we will probably go to Northwest River Post, get dogs and provisions, and snowshoe S.W. to Natishquan or some such point. If we don't get to the caribou grounds in time—well, we'll have to get some fish ahead, or use our pea meal in a dash for the George River H.B.C. Post. After breakfast George and I went in rain to climb mountain. No water into S.W. bay of our lake as we hoped. Trolling back, I caught one small namaycush. Then we all started to hunt for a rapid we heard on the south side of this lake. Caught one 2 1/2 lb. namaycush. Found rapid. Good sized stream falling in from south. Big hopes, but too shoal and rapid, no pools. Only one mess of trout. Very much disappointed. While Wallace and I fish, George gone to troll. When he gets back, we will go to look for inlet into Low's "Northwest River." Not finding that we will start on a portage for it in the morning. Later by camp fire. Weather has cleared. All bright and starry. Caught a 7-lb. namaycush and so we eat to-night.

Saturday, September 12th.—Temp. 38 degrees. High N.W. wind. Clouds and clear by spells. Dashes of snow. We camped on a little island not far from the N.E. main land where we hope inlet is, just at dusk. Ate big namaycush and were ready to push on early this morning. Two meals of trout ahead. Awoke this A.M. to find awful gale stirring the lake to fury. No leaving. Wallace and I stayed in tent mending. I made pair of moccasins out of a pair of seal mittens and some old sacking. Patched a pair of socks with duffel. Not comfortable, but will do. George went to canoe to get fish. "That's too bad," said he. "What?" I asked. "Somebody's taken the trout." "Who?" "Don't know. Otter or carcajou, maybe." And sure enough they were gone—our day's grub. We all laughed—there was nothing else to do. So we had some thin soup, made with three thin slices of bacon in a big pot of water and just a bit of flour and rice stirred in. One felt rather hungrier after eating it, but then we did not suffer or get weak. It is very disappointing to be delayed like this; but we can only make the most of it and wait. No game or fish on this island and no hopes of getting off till it calms. So we are cheerful, and make the most of a good rest and a chance to mend; and we need both, though perhaps we need progress more.

Sunday, September 13th.—Temp. 39 degrees 5 A.M. High N.W. wind in A.M. Clear, rain, sleet by spells. Heavy wind continued this A.M. Some more rice and bacon soup for breakfast. Read Philemon aloud and told story of it. Also 1st and 91st Psalm. Found blue berries, and all ate. At about one o'clock, wind dropped somewhat. We started to hunt outlet into N.W. River, supposed to be N.E. of island. N.G. Shot at goose—missed. Hooked big namaycush—lost it. Caught another 6 lbs. Ate it for lunch about 4 P.M. Picked gallon of cranberries. Ate a pot stewed with a little flour for supper. Enough for two meals left. Not very satisfactory, but lots better than nothing. Sat long by camp fire.

Monday, September 14th.—Temp. 40 degrees 5 A.M. High N.W. wind, clear and showers by spells. Very much disappointed to find heavy gale blowing. Could not leave shore. Had breakfast of very thin soup. Then all slept till nearly noon. I dreamed again of being home. Hungry all day. George and I have decided that we must not start this way home before freezing up time. Might get caught again by bad winds. Better freeze on the George River with the Indians, save grub if we get any, and then snowshoe clear out. Later by camp fire. Hard to keep off depression to-night. Wind continues and all hungry.

Tuesday, September 15th.—Temp. 31 degrees 5 A.M. West wind, spits of sleet, and fair. Wind continued hard all day. Could not leave shore. I lay awake all last night thinking over situation. George is worried and talks of Indians who starve. Tries to be cheerful but finds it hard. Here we are, wind bound, long way from Michikamau, no hopes of wind abating. The caribou migration is due to begin, yet we can't start and are at least two weeks from their grounds, with no grub and no prospect of good weather. Our grub is 18 lbs. pea meal, to be held for emergency, and 2 lbs. of flour,

122

1 pint rice, 3 lbs. bacon. To go on is certain failure to reach the caribou killing, and probable starvation. If we turn back we must stop and get grub, then cross our long portage, then hunt more grub, and finally freeze up preparatory to a sled dash for Northwest River. That will make us late for boat, but we can snowshoe to the St. Lawrence. All this, with what we have done so far, will make a bully story. I don't see anything better to do. I asked Wallace. He opposed and then said it was best. I said to George, "Would you rather go on or turn back?" "I came to go with you, and I want to do what you do." When I said we will turn back he was very greatly pleased. Now my job is to get the party back to Northwest River, getting grub as we go. We will take the back track to some good fishing grounds, catch fish, try to kill a caribou, and wait for freeze. We can't take the canoe down the Nascaupee. Hence the need of freezing. Stayed in camp all day. Could not launch canoe. No place to fish or hunt. Feel better now that the decision is made. Ate very thin rice and bacon soup and drank tea. Long chat with Wallace. Feeling good in spite of short grub. George is telling again how be will visit his sister at Flying Post and what be will eat. We are talking of plans for our home-going, and are happy despite impending hunger.

Wednesday, September 16th.—Temp. 29 degrees 6 A.M. Wind N.W. Shifting to N.E. Little rain. Moved to rapid on south shore where there is some trout fishing, and hard place to be wind bound. Must fish a few days and get grub ahead for our long portage back to Namaycush Lake. Ate last bit of bacon at noon, cut in three pieces and boiled with rice and a little flour. Boys trolled in P.M. I made camp and fished brook. Too cold. They lost two good namaycush. I took two 10-inch trout. Boiled these into a mush and put last handful of rice and a little flour into pot with them. Good soup. Made us feel stronger.

Thursday, September 17th.—Temp. 33 degrees 6 A.M. Rained all last night and all this P.M. For breakfast a whisky jack, stewed with flour and about two spoonfuls of erbswurst. Good. Wallace and I each had half a bird. If we get enough fish ahead to take us across this portage, our pea meal and what fish we can get on river will see us to the post. Hoping weather will improve so we can make a good haul. Disheartening in extreme to be working all the time in rain and wind and cold. I made a map this A.M. of our long portage—about 30 miles. Will require about seven days. Wallace and I stretched tarpaulin by fire and sat long beneath it chatting. Wallace is a great comfort these evenings. There has been no friction this trip whatever. I think I'll get a bully story out of it despite our failure to find the Nascaupees. I'll get more in freezing up, more in Northwest River people and more in the winter journey to God's country.

Friday, September 18th.—Temp. 38 degrees 6 A.M. S.E. wind, turning to N.W. gale about noon. Raw and snow by spells. Caught three namaycush in AM., then wind bound by fierce N.W. gale at camp. Wallace caught 2 1/2 lbs. trout. I caught 1 lb. Namaycush heads and guts and my trout for supper. Boiled with last of flour. Hungry and a bit weak, but all cheerful. Sat late by roaring camp fire. Very depressing this, getting wind bound so often just when we are trying to get fish ahead for our long portage towards home. Have thought a good deal about home. It seems to me I'll never be willing to leave it again. I don't believe I'll want any more trips too hard for M. to share. Her companionship and our home life are better than a great trip. So it seems to me.

Saturday, September 19th.—Rain and snow last night, temp. 32 degrees. Gale from northwest all day. Wind bound in camp all day. Lay in tent almost all the time. Spits of snow. No breakfast. Bit of fish and its liquor for lunch. Same with a dash of pea meal at night. Oh! to be away from this lake and its gales and to be started home! Last night we quit rolling in blankets and made bed to keep warm. All three crawled in. Warmer than other way. Quite comfortable all night. Plan a great deal for the future. I am planning to give more time to home. Less fretting and more home life. I've let my ambitions worry me. More time for my meals when I get home and more for my wife and our friends. I want to give one or two little dinners in the woods when we get back and while George is there. A turkey roast like a goose. Stuffed. Potatoes, bannocks, made while the turkey is roasting, one of George's puddings, coffee and maple cream.

Sunday, September 20th.—Temp. 6 A.M. 29 degrees. Morning bright and clear. Light N.W. wind. Showers in P.M. Squally. To-night we are starting for Northwest River Post. When we reach the big river we can I think nearly live on the fish we get there. From there too, there are more signs of caribou. About four days more and we ought to reach a remnant of flour we threw away. It was wet and lumpy, but we will welcome it now. It, if it is usable, will see us to the head of Grand Lake, where Skipper Blake has a cache, I think, in a winter hunting shanty. It promises to be a hungry trip, but it is a man's game. Now that we are starting home I am content with the trip and the material. We've done all we could. Our minds turn to home even more and we are anxious to be back. So hungry to see all the old friends.

Tuesday, September 22nd.—Temp. 38 degrees. N.W. wind. Rain in morning and by spells all day. All feel stronger today than yesterday. Tried to stalk goose in bad swamp. Missed at long range. Waded above knees in mud and water to get shot. Portaged all day mostly through low or swampy ground. Happy to be going home. Camped tonight on second old camping-ground. George and Wallace brought up outfit while I made camp and got wood.

Wednesday, September 23rd.—Rain by spells. W. wind. Clear in evening and cold. Portaged all day. Crossed barren ridge. Had big feed of moss-berries and cranberries. Wallace had apparent tea sickness and vomited. Erbswurst same as yesterday. Feel quite weak to-night. Had carried canoe a good deal. A good deal depressed till camp fire. Then good again. Bright, crisp night. Dried clothing and got warm. Talked long by fire of home. Blankets very damp. Hard time keeping warm at night.

Thursday, September 24th.—Temp. 28 degrees. N.E. wind. Snowing in morning. Quite cold last night, but clear and crisp till toward morning when it snowed. Blankets very damp, but by drying clothes at fire and getting good and warm, we slept warm and well. Dreamed M. and I were at Missanabie. How I do wish I could

124

see her again at home. Thinking too much maybe, about home now. Makes too big contrast. Snow covered ground by noon. Disagreeable morning, but a little crisp wintriness helped it some. Plodded along on a pea soup breakfast, wondering what the outcome will be—a little. Nasty weather makes one wonder—and thinking of M. and home. Then came a happy event. George had said last night be could kill a wild goose this A.M. if I would let him take rifle. Did so, half convinced by his confidence, and knowing he was a big goose shooter down on "The Bay." He had started ahead. Had seen flock light in pond ahead. Wallace and I heard four shots. Came to where George had left pack. He was coming with no goose. "You can kick me," said he, "but I got a goose." We took canoe to his pond. He had killed one goose, which was drifting ashore, and wounded another, which sat on shore and let George end it with a pistol. Never was goose more gladly received I'll venture. I promised George two cook-books and a dinner as a reward.

Friday, September 25th.—Temp. 28 degrees. Wind N.E. Snow squalls. Half goose breakfast. Pea soup, thin, for dinner. Half goose, supper. Goose is bully. When done eating we burn the bones and chew them. Nasty day. Portaged to old camp on small lake and stopped. All day I have been thinking about childhood things and the country. I want to get into touch with it again. I want to go to Canada, if possible, for Christmas. I want to go somewhere in sugar making. So homesick for my sweetheart. Fairly strong despite short grub.

Saturday, September 26th.—Temp. 28 degrees. Wind N.E. Rain in early morning, cold wind, warming in late P.M. Clear at mid-day. Dried blankets. Travelled over our old course to our "long-lake-that-looks-like-a-river." Shot a large duck's head off with rifle. Had hopes of a few fish at place where we found them spawning on our westward way, but was fearful of the cold. Left George cooking and went to try with Wallace's rod, not over hopeful, as water was very high and weather cold. Delighted to catch twenty very fair ones while lunch was cooking. In P.M. took ninety-five more. Estimated weight of catch 70 pounds. We will stay here to-morrow and dry fish for journey. This is a wonderful relief. It means enough fish to put us through to our big lake, or nearly so. We had no hopes of such a catch, and would have been delighted with just a meal or two. Then it means, I hope, that we will find the trout biting at other spawning places, and catch enough to live on in spite of the cold weather. We are happier than for weeks before for we believe this almost guarantees our safe return home. Rain drove us from our camp fire just after George had declared, "Now we'll talk about French toast, and what we'll eat when we get to New York." So we all crawled into blankets and did plan and plan good dinners.

Sunday, September 27th.—Warm day, partly clear, wind S.W. Ate last of goose for breakfast. Bully.

Monday, September 28th.—Snow and clear by spells. Stayed in camp to rest and feed up. Were all weak as cats when we relaxed from the grub strain. We kept smoke going under stage and lay in tent most of day. Boiled fish for breakfast, roast smoked fish for other meals. Like them rather better the latter way.

Tuesday, September 29th.—Temp. 24 degrees. Snow by squalls all day. Wind W. Caught twelve good trout while boys were breaking camp. Diarrhoea, which attacked me yesterday, came back when I started to carry the canoe. Had to drop it and became very weak. Boys went on with it about 1 1/4 miles and came back. We camped on long lake. I huddled by fire and wrote when it was not snowing. We can catch up to our schedule if I am able to travel to-morrow for it is only an easy march, covered in less than a day before. All talking about home, all happy to be going there.

Wednesday, September 30th.—Boys carried canoe nearly to Pike Lake, while I made camp and went back and forth three times to bring up packs. Then a happy camp nearer home. To-night we planned, in case we have a long wait in St. John's to get rooms for light housekeeping and not go to hotel. Then we can cook what we want and need and live high—beef bones for caribou, cereals with real cream, rich muscle-making stews of rice, beef, *etc.*, tomatoes, *etc.*

Thursday, October 1st.—Temp. 40 degrees. Crossed to Pike Lake this A.M. Lunch on west side, last of fish. Nothing now left but pea meal. Crossed lake, no trail on east side, hoping to get trout where I took a mess in outlet coming up. Not a nibble. Too cold or something. Camped in lee of trees. Boys had feed of blue berries while I fished. Ate half stick of erbswurst. Good camp-fire, but I rather blue and no one talkative. So hungry for home— and fish.

Friday, October 2nd.—Cold west wind. Temp. 30 degrees. Cold— snowed a bit in the evening. Took packs early in day and hurried across to tamarack pole fishing place. Only two trout before noon. Ate them with pea meal and boys went back for the canoe. Only two days, and easy ones, to our big lake. Then only two days to the river with its good fishing. That makes us feel good. It means a good piece nearer home.

Saturday, October 3rd.—Bright crisp morning. Temp. 21 degrees. Snow squalls. Left tamarack pole place and portaged south over old route, crossing lakes, *etc.*, to our camp of 29th August, on little pond. Wet feet and cold, but not a bad day. I lugged all the packs and boys canoe. Beautiful moon and clear night. All sat late by camp fire talking and thinking of home. Pleased to have another fair march back of us—happy.

Sunday, October 4th.—Temp. 10 degrees. Bright clear cold A.M. Everything frozen in morning. Pond frozen over. Two trout left. One for breakfast, boiled with erbswurst. Portaged to lake about three-quarter mile away. Crossed it. Some ice to annoy. George borrowed Wallace's pistol saying he saw a partridge. He killed four. Lord's with us. We need 'em bad. I'm weak and nervous. Must have vacation. Wallace notices it. Have not taken bath for two weeks, ashamed of my ribs which stick out like skeletons.

Monday, October 5th.—Temp. 30 degrees. Wind S.E. Snow on the ground. Up late. Waited Wallace to mend moccasins. Late start. Crossed bad swamp to big

126

lake, wading icy water. Dried feet and drank cup soup. Stopped island in P.M. to get berries. All talk much of home now. At camp fire George told me of his plans to get married and his love story.

Tuesday, October 6th.—Temp. 48 degrees. Rain and snow in A.M. George shot partridge before breakfast. Rained most of night. Started expecting to portage to lake first west of Height of Land. Got into rough sea, exciting time. Found river of considerable size emptying into that lake. Ran into it and prepared to finish in the morning. George and I ran on rock shooting rapid. Beautiful night—cold. Feel all cold.

Wednesday, October 7th.—Thermometer out of order. Heavy frost. Ran down river into lake, west of barren mountain, climbed to scout on day after entering lake W. of Height of Land. Stopped and fed well on our moss berries and cranberries. Took some along. Started Height of Land portage. Happy to be back. Very thin pea soup breakfast. Some with berries for lunch. Weak.

Thursday, October 8th.—Thermometer N.G. Very frosty. Dreamed last night we were going out of bush, very weak and hungry. Came to our old Michigan Farm and found mother. Wonder where mother is now. Do want a vacation at home or in Canada. May be won't need it after ride on steamer. Finished Height of Land portage and came on to place where we dried caribou (second time), at head of Ptarmigan Lake. I caught four fish, small trout, while Wallace was going back for rifle, which he had left at far end of small lake. Wallace came back with partridge. This delayed us and we did not reach good fishing rapid. Hoped to get trout there. Did catch a few before—failed to-night. Bright crisp day too. George very blue in consequence. Wallace and I not worried. Pea meal down to less than two pounds. No other food save tea. Thinking much of home and M., and our plans and old friends. I want to keep better in touch with relatives everywhere and the country. How I wish for that vacation in Michigan or Canada! or a good quiet time at Congers, and I am aching to write home sketches and stories that have come to my mind. We talk much of future plans, and the camp fire continues to be a glorious meeting place.

Friday, October 9th.—Reached good fishing hole at rapid where we caught so many trout on way up. Got about fifty in P.M. Glorious, crisp fall day. Dried blankets. Fifteen trout lunch; twelve supper; then six roast before bedtime. Disappointing. Hoped for some to dry. Only one day's slim fish ahead—one and a half pounds pea meal. No hopes of getting ahead fish to freeze up. Must get out to civilisation. Pretty weak all of us.

Saturday, October 10th.—From rapid about half way to Camp Caribou. Boys shot rapids while I fished. Beautiful day till about noon. Then cloudy and cold west wind. Cheerful camp fire as always. About twenty trout, nine boiled for supper. Same for lunch. Much talk of grub and restaurants, and our home going, much of George's room in New York, of good days in Congers. I want to go to Michigan and Canada and to Wurtsboro'. Oh, to see my sweetheart and be home again!

Sunday, October 11th.—Beautiful, clear day, cold. Off day for grub. George shot three times at ducks and I fished at rapids. No fish—no ducks. Nine small trout breakfast, eight lunch. No supper ahead save what George hoped to find at Camp Caribou. Arrived there tired and weak about an hour before sunset. George gathered bones and two hoofs. Pounded part of them up. Maggots on hoofs. We did not mind. Boiled two kettlefuls of hoofs and bones. Made a good greasy broth. We had three cupfuls each and sat about gnawing bones. Got a good deal of gristle from the bones, and some tough hide and gristly stuff from hoofs. I enjoyed it and felt like a square meal. Ate long, as it is a slow tough job. Saved the bones to boil over.

Monday, October 12th.—Made about 9 miles to-day. Several bad rapids. Shot them. George and I nearly came to grief in one. My fault. Beautiful day. Fished a little, but no fish bit. Hope to leave stream to-morrow, and that makes us happy. For breakfast bones of caribou boiled to make greasy broth. Quite supply of grease in it. Hoofs too boiled. Some gristle to these that was good. Strong, rancid taste, but we relished it. Roasted hard part of hoofs in fire, ate them. Half rubber, half leather, but heap better than nothing. For lunch the same with skin from velvet horns added. Latter boiled up and was very good. At night some bones boiled to make broth, skin from head added. Part of mine I could eat boiled. Part from nose very thick and had to be roasted first. Good. Sat by camp fire long time. Very sleepy. Talked of home and friends and grub and plans.

Tuesday, October 13th.—Lightened our packs a bit, throwing away more or less useless stuff at old shack, where we had a rainy night. Pot of tea at Rainy Sunday Camp. All very hungry and weak. Camped below Rainy Sunday Camp. Tried wenastica, not bad. Not much taste to it. Thinking all time of home and M. and parents and Congers and Wurtsboro' and childhood and country.

Wednesday, October 14th.—Caribou bones, boiled into broth for breakfast. Then George shot a duck. Came back. "Lord surely guided that bullet," said he reverently. He had killed a wonderfully fat duck. Oh! but it was good and greasy. Made bully lunch boiled, and good pot of broth. Left river where we entered it. Left canoe, sextant box, artificial horizon and my fishing-rod. Packs still too heavy for our strength. Little progress. Reached old camp where we left lakes for big river. Hoped fish. No bites. Cold east wind. Big fire. All cheerful. Just bone broth and a bit of wenastica for supper. Must lighten packs to limit. Count on bit of flour 22 miles from here. Here George found two old goose heads and some bones we left. Saved them for breakfast. All gnawed some charred bones. George found three tiny slices of bacon in old lard can we left—one each. How good they were. The scrapings of lard he melted for the broth pot. We have 1 1/6 lbs. pea meal left. No other grub but tea. We think this will take us to our bit of flour, if it is still left, and Blake has a cache, we think, at the head of Grand Lake about 24 miles beyond that. Hope to get out O.K. Count on berries to help us. Had some moss berries to-day.

Thursday, October 15th.—Dreamed last night came to New York, found M. and had my first meal with her. How I hated to find it a dream. Lightened packs a good deal. Left Wallace's rifle, cartridges, rod, my cleaning rod, my sextant and 15 films and other things, cached in bushes at left side of little stream between two lakes. Wallace hated to leave his rifle, I hated to leave other stuff. Spent most of forenoon getting ready. Ate for breakfast bit of skin from old caribou head, boiled with bone broth. At lunch on Montagnais Lake, same, but skin was from old caribou hide, which we had carried to mend moccasins. Were almost to our second camp where we ate first goose, when I got shaky and busted and had to stop. Wallace came back and got my pack and I walked to camp unloaded. In P.M. George shot three partridges which jumped up before us in a swamp. Killed them with my pistol. Made us very happy. Ate one for supper, OH! how good. In spite of my weakness I was happy to-night. I remember a similar happiness once after I went to New York. I got caught in rain, had no car fare, got soaked, spent last 10 cents for rolls and crullers, then crawled into bed to get dry and eat, not knowing where the next meal would come from. Talk of home. George not thinking now of eating of recent years, but just the things his mother used to make for him as a child. Same way with Wallace and me, save that I think of what M. and I have eaten that she made.

Sunday, October 18th.—Alone in camp—junction of Nascaupee and some other stream—estimated (overestimated I hope) distance above head of Grand Lake, 33 miles. For two days past we have travelled down our old trail with light packs. We left a lot of flour wet— about 11 miles below here, 12 miles (approximately) below that about a pound of milk powder, 4 miles below that about 4 pounds of lard. We counted on all these to help us out in our effort to reach the head of Grand Lake where we hoped to find Skipper Tom Blake's trapping camp and cache. On Thursday as stated, I busted. Friday and Saturday it was the same. I saw it was probably useless for me to try to go farther with the boys, so we counselled last night, and decided they should take merely half a blanket each, socks, *etc.*, some tea, tea pail, cups, and the pistols, and go on. They will try to reach the flour to-morrow. Then Wallace will bring a little and come back to me. George will go on to the milk and lard and to Skipper Blake if he can, and send or lead help to us. I want to say here that they are two of the very best, bravest, and grandest men I ever knew, and if I die it will not be because they did not put forth their best efforts. Our past two days have been trying ones. I have not written my diary because so very weak. Day before yesterday we caught sight of a caribou, but it was on our lee, and, winding us, got away before a shot could be fired.

Yesterday at an old camp, we found the end we had cut from a flour bag. It had a bit of flour sticking to it. We boiled it with our old caribou bones and it thickened the broth a little. We also found a can of mustard we had thrown away. I sat and held it in my hand a long time, thinking how it came from Congers and our home, and what a happy home it was. Then I took a bite of it and it was very good. We mixed some in our bone broth and it seemed to stimulate us. We had a bit of caribou skin in the same pot. It swelled thick and was very good. Last night I fell asleep while the boys were reading to me. This morning I was very, very sleepy. After the boys left—they left me tea, the caribou bones, and another end of flour sack found here, a rawhide caribou moccasin, and some yeast cakes—I drank a cup of strong tea and some bone broth. I also ate some of the really delicious rawhide, boiled with the bones, and it made me stronger—strong to write this. The boys have only tea and one half pound pea meal (erbswurst). Our parting was most affecting. I did not feel so bad. George said, "The Lord help us, Hubbard. With His help I'll save you if I can get out." Then he cried. So did Wallace. Wallace stooped and kissed my cheek with his poor, sunken, bearded lips several times— and I kissed George did the same, and I kissed his cheek. Then they went away. God bless and help them.

I am not so greatly in doubt as to the outcome. I believe they will reach the flour and be strengthened, that Wallace will reach me, that George will find Blake's cache and camp and send help. So I believe we will all get out.

My tent is pitched in open tent style in front of a big rock. The rock reflects the fire, but now it is going out because of the rain. I think I shall let it go and close the tent, till the rain is over, thus keeping out wind and saving wood. To-night or to-morrow perhaps the weather will improve so I can build a fire, eat the rest of my moccasins and have some bone broth. Then I can boil my belt and oil-tanned moccasins and a pair of cowhide mittens. They ought to help some. I am not suffering. The acute pangs of hunger have given way to indifference. I am sleepy. I think death from starvation is not so bad. But let no one suppose that I expect it. I am prepared, that is all. I think the boys will be able with the Lord's help to save me.

NARRATIVE BY GEORGE ELSON

LAST DAYS TOGETHER

Friday, October 9th.—We got up good and early. Only tea we had, expecting when we got to our rapid to have something to eat. After going about 2 miles we came to our old camp where we camped on our way up where we had a goose that Mr. Hubbard had killed. I also had killed one. We went ashore to see if we could find some of the old bones. We gathered all we could find and ate them all.

Mr. Hubbard said, "I often have seen dogs eating bones and thought it was pretty hard lines for them, but it must be only fun for them."

Before coming to our rapid, the rapid we had always talked about where we thought we would get lots of fish, I told Mr. Hubbard and Wallace my dream I had that night. It did not seem like a dream but more like some one talking to me. When travelling this summer when we began to be out of grub, if we dreamt of having a good meal at some restaurant we often told it to each other next morning. This morning my dream was:—

A man came to me and told me, "You will get to the rapid to-day and I cannot spare you more than two or three meals of fish, and do not waste much time there. Go right on and don't leave the river, but follow the river on. It is only the way you can save your lives. Follow the river down."

We got to the rapid about noon, all feeling very, very weak. I started a fire. By the time I got some wood and had my fire started they had already enough fish for a pretty fair meal and, of course, you can imagine how glad we were and did not delay much time but got our fish for lunch. It was nice to have something to eat again. We were pretty sure of getting lots more. After lunch Mr. Hubbard and Wallace fished. It was good signs of caribou round there. I took the rifle and tracked up the caribou, but I saw nothing. It was late when I got back. The boys were still fishing. They had caught about sixty more little trout. We felt as if we could eat all those fish in one meal, but seeing they were so scarce we had to try and save some for the next day.

Saturday, October 10th.—We fished all before noon and did not get any at all. So we had to start off from there, seeing it was no use in trying to fish any more. We came to some more rapids in the afternoon. Wallace and I ran some with empty canoe, and then went back for our dunnage, while Mr. Hubbard would fish. It got very cold in the afternoon. Mr. Hubbard caught about twenty little trout. Looking forward we hoped next day to get to our old camp, Camp Caribou, where we killed our caribou August 12th. We thought that may be we will find some of the old bones so as to make some broth, thinking it would help us some. We camped just near the river where we could get lots of wood, and have a good camp fire so we could sit beside the camp fire and have a good talk about home.

131

Mr. Hubbard tells me he will get a room for me in New York. He again that night asked me to stay with him a couple of months in Congers before I go home to Missanabie, and also to pay him a visit real often, and also that he would never go out doing any travelling without me.

He said, "I am sure Mrs. Hubbard will not be able to do enough for you, especially when she knows how good you have been to me. I would like to have you come with me to Michigan. I am sure my sister would like to have you tell them the story about our trip."

Sunday, October 11th.—Had four small trout for lunch, only little larger than a sardine. Late in the evening we came to our old camp, where we had the caribou. Most of the bones were carried off by some animals. Picked up all we could find and made some broth, and very, very strong broth too, which I suppose no one could hardly believe that any human being could eat. The bones were full of maggots, and when it boiled for some time the maggots would boil out. It just looked like if it had been little rice in it. We drunk it up maggots and all. It was pretty high, but found it good. Nothing was too bad for us to eat.

Monday, October 12th.—Fine day. In the morning we had bone broth again and tea. We started off carrying all the bones we could find in our pail, also taking the caribou horns with us. At noon we had broth and piece of the hide we got off from the caribou horns. In the evening we came to a rapid. Hubbard and I nearly swamped the canoe, and part of the rapid was too rough to run. It was only just a short lift over, about 100 feet. The three of us took the canoe, and before getting over we dropped it. We were getting so weak that it took the three of us to carry the canoe, and yet we couldn't even that distance. We looked at each other, but none complained of his weakness. We found we could not go any farther without something to eat. We ate one of Mr. Hubbard's old moccasins, made out of caribou skin, that he made himself. We boiled it in the frying pan, till it got kind of soft, and we shared in three parts. Each had his share and found it good, and also drank up the water where it was boiled in. At night we had some tea, and it freshened us up some.

Tuesday, October 13th.—Wind raw and cold. We came to a little fall we had to carry over, quite short, about 40 feet portage, but our canoe we hadn't the strength to carry. We had to drag it over the rocks.

I shot a whisky jack, and we had it along with our bone broth and tea. Not knowing what our next meal would be, or whether we will ever have the pleasure of enjoying another meal, it looked very much like starvation.

My back was aching quite a bit that day. Touch of lumbago. It made things worse for me. I thought it would be impossible for me to try and go any farther. So I told Mr. Hubbard that if I did not feel any better in the morning, they could go on and try to make their way out and leave me behind, because I did not want to delay them in the least. For all, I was sure they would never make their way out; but I thought they might try anyway. Mr. Hubbard was very, very sorry about it; but he said he hoped I'd be better in the morning.

Wednesday, October 14th.—The boys were up before me and had a fire on. It was some time before I could get up; but I was feeling better than I did the night before. Before noon I shot a duck with the rifle. We were very happy boys.

At noon we came to the place where we had planned some time ago to leave the canoe and cross over to the Nascaupee again. We had our nice duck for lunch, and enjoyed it very much. Mr. Hubbard then asked me if I could find the flour we had thrown away some time in July, along the Nascaupee.

"Yes," I said, "if no animal has carried it away. It is over 20 miles from here."

"Then," he said, "I think we better leave the canoe and march over to the Nascaupee."

And the reason why I did not try and persuade him more than I did for us not to leave the Big River was, we thought perhaps there would be lots of places where we could not run our canoe in some wild rapids, and would have to carry our canoe. I knew the last two days how we were when trying to carry our canoe, and we also thought that if we were travelling through the bush we would surely come across some partridges and help us to the flour, and the flour would help us to the lard, about three pounds, and some milk and coffee 3 miles from Grand Lake. Also as we only know the river above there, of course, we did not know where the river ran to. The boys thought it ran out to Goose Bay, as Low's map showed only the one river running into Grand Lake. Also at Rigolette, trying to find out all we could, and at Northwest River too, nobody ever said about any river but the Nascaupee. Still I said it might run out into Grand Lake.

So the canoe, one axe, the sextant box, and the rest of the caribou horns we left; but the bones we carried with us in our pail, which we boiled over and over to make broth. The bones, since we had them, we would scorch in the fire at night, and chew away at them. Was pretty hard chewing.

I told the boys when we decided to leave the canoe, that we had better leave everything we have, so we would make better time; but we didn't want to waste any time after our nice duck, but go right on while we have yet some strength from it. So we didn't wait to overhaul our stuff. We traveled 2 miles from the Big River that afternoon. We found our packs too heavy to carry, and decided to lighten up in the morning.

That evening Mr. Hubbard said, "Mrs. Hubbard this evening will be now at dinner, and after her meal will finish with lot more on the table. Oh, if she could only hand me a piece of bread!"

Thursday morning, October 15th.—We threw away lots of dunnage, also some films and one rifle. Mr. Hubbard was very sorry to leave his flask. He had often spoken of it being a present from Mrs. Hubbard.

I shot three partridges after noon with the pistol. We were so glad. Mr. Hubbard was more than glad. He came and shook hands with me.

We were trying to reach our old camping place on our way up, Goose Camp we called it, but we were all feeling so very weak especially Mr. Hubbard. At last he could not go any farther. I told him it was about 40 yards to where our old camp was. So we made him leave his load and he followed us. I, with the greatest hurry, started a fire and made him a cup of tea. We as usual sat up near our fire for some time, trying to encourage each other about what good things we would have, after we got to New York.

Friday, October 16th.—For breakfast we ate one partridge leaving the other for lunch. Threw more things away, one blanket and more films, and at noon more things left behind. I had a good suit of underwear with me, saving it till cold weather, but that day at noon I left everything belonging to me. I was too weak to take off the bad and put on the good. Also left some films and—came to the Nascaupee.

That day just before noon, we came to a place where Mr. Hubbard had caught some fish when we were going up, and we thought that perhaps we could get some fish there again, but the little stream was nearly dry. We sat down and had a rest.

A little lake about 400 Yards from us on our way. This little stream ran into the lake. Just near the lake I saw a caribou coming along following this little river to where we were.

I told the boys, "There's a caribou coming along."

We all fell flat on the ground; but he was on the lee side of us and soon found out we were there. He stood—behind some little trees and had his head up looking towards where we were, and all of a sudden he was gone, and we didn't have the chance to fire. I got up. A swamp I knew of. I made for that swamp thinking I would cut across him. I tried to run, yet I was so very, very weak. Oh! how hard I tried to run. But when I got out there he was across on the other side. I was away for some time, yet when I came to the boys, they were still lain the same way, and their faces to the ground, and did not move till I spoke to them. We were more than sorry about the caribou, and each one said what he would do, and how much we could eat if we killed that caribou and that we would stay right there for a few days till we got a little stronger.

Though I was feeling so very weak myself, when we would have nothing else but tea, as we often just had tea, nothing else, when I would hand the boys a cup of tea each, I would ask them to pass it back, as I would pretend I'd forgotten to put any sugar in. They would pretend that they didn't care for sugar, and refuse to have some. Then I would ask them if they would have some bread or some pie.

Mr. Hubbard would say, "PIE! What is pie? What do they use it for? Do they eat it?"

This I did often to encourage them and myself, that we might forget the danger ahead; but it was something impossible to forget, as the hunger and weakness pained us, and I thought we would not be able to go many more days if we don't succeed in killing anything.

That evening we hadn't the strength of chopping our wood. Just gathered the small, dry pieces we found near our camp. We also put up our camp in an easy way we thought. Three little poles were required to keep up our tent. They were quite handy; but it took me some time before I could cut them down.

That day at noon, when I left my dunnage bag with lots of films in, and hung the bag on a short stump, Mr. Hubbard told me, "If we get out safe to Northwest River, I think you or I might stay there this winter, and try and get out some of the things we are leaving, especially the films. If we could get out in time of the last trip of the *Virginia Lake*, Wallace and you could go home. Or if you would stay, Wallace and I could go home."

I told him I would be very much in a hurry to go home, and wouldn't wish to stay out here for the winter. "But if you wish, and rather have me stay, I will stay for the winter and try and get the things out for you."

He was so glad about it and said, "It will be better, of course, if you would stay, as you could make a better guess for the things than I would."

Saturday, October 17th.—We followed the river, and without anything to eat all day. Only tea we had. Sometimes we would be completely done out. Then we would make some tea and help us some and start on again. This we kept on doing all day.

That evening we came to the junction of the river where it branches off. About half an hour before we came to the branch we had a fire, as Mr. Hubbard was feeling cold and chilly all day. Just at the forks we found a few red berries, and to see if I could find some more I just went about 20 yards from them. When I found none and returned to see them, Mr. Hubbard was lying down on the damp rocks and moss. He looked so pitiful and Wallace sitting near him. I told him not to lie on the damp moss, and asked him if I'd better make him a cup of tea.

"Yes," he said, "I think if I had a cup of hot tea I'd feel better and then go on again."

135

He could hardly speak. I knew he was very weak. I asked him if he could get to where we camped before going up, where it was nice and dry, about 20 yards. He said he would try. I took his and my pack and he followed us. He could just barely walk. We made him a place near the fire, and gave him a cup of hot tea, and made him a cup of pea meal.

We put the camp up the best way we could and gathered enough wood to last all night.

The flour we were coming for was yet 10 miles away, and the advance in covering so many miles each day, became less and less each day. So after we had some tea and bone broth, I thought, seeing it was no use trying to keep it to ourselves any longer, the danger before us, I would tell them what was in my mind (not about restaurants this time) before it was too late. Seeing that death was just near, which anyone else, if in our place, would expect nothing else but death, they were quite satisfied and each did the same.

Mr. Hubbard talked about Mrs. Hubbard, and his father and mother, and his brother and sister, but most about Mrs. Hubbard. Wallace talked of his sisters and I did the same, especially my youngest brother, as my father and mother died some years ago and he was left under my care. It was quite a different talk beside the other nights' talk, as we never let a night pass without being talking about good restaurants, and what we would do when we got home.

About 10 miles from there the flour was we were looking forward to. So I told Mr. Hubbard to see what he would think. If he couldn't really have the strength of going any farther, that Wallace and I would try and go and find the flour, and if we found it one would return and bring some of the flour to him, and the other would try and make his way out to Northwest River, as it is nearly 80 miles to Northwest River post, and may be I might come across some trappers and be able to help him.

He at first said it was no use of trying, as he knew how weak we were and that we would only be scattered abroad.

Should a relief party be sent out to look for us, they will find us here in our camp; but if you wish to try all right. You are more than trying to save me. I never came across a man so brave as you are. Still I may feel better in the morning, and I will not carry anything. Now I see that you were right when we left the canoe. You wanted to leave everything and go out light.

If you get to the flour, you must take most of the flour and Wallace will bring the rest. As we will be staying in one place we will not require as much as you will, because if you fail on the way, it will mean sure death to us too. And if you happen to come on some trappers, just send them with grub, and don't come up yourself as you will be too weak. Or if you get to Northwest River, Mr. M'Kenzie will find men to send, and you will stay there. If I should starve and you get out, Mr. M'Kenzie will help you in all you need, and will keep you there this winter. By the first boat you will go to New York, and my diary don't give to anyone but to Mrs. Hubbard. Tell her how things happened, and that I don't suffer now as I did at first, only so very, very weak, and I think starvation is an easy death to die.

"I wish you could only see my father and mother, or my sister, so as to tell them about our trip. I wish I could tell them how good you were to me. But you must go to Mrs. Hubbard.

"I am sorry, boys. It is my work the reason why you are out here. If I did not come out here you would have been at your home and having all that you need and would not meet death so soon."

I told him not to be troubled by that. "If we didn't want to come we could have stayed at home. So don't put the blame on yourself."

He also told Wallace if he got out to write the story for Mrs. Hubbard.

Mr. Hubbard was very sleepy. So we did not sit up so long as we have done before. Mr. Wallace read three chapters to us. Mr. Hubbard chose thirteenth chapter First Corinthians, and I the seventeenth chapter St. John's Gospel, and Mr. Wallace fourteenth chapter St. John. Mr. Hubbard fell asleep when Mr. Wallace was nearly through reading the second chapter, that is, the seventeenth chapter. Mr. Hubbard slept good all night, and hardly ever moved till morning, when I wakened him and gave him a cup of hot tea and some bone broth. I also slept good all night and didn't hardly wake up till just before daylight. Mr. Wallace kept on a fire all night and wrote a farewell letter to his sisters.

Sunday morning, October 18th, I got up and boiled those bones again, putting in just a little of the pea meal in the broth, and also tea we had for breakfast. We had yet a half pound of the pea meal that we had carried for some time.

We were to start early, and seeing Mr. Hubbard still weaker than he was last night, and was not able to go any farther, it was late when we started. We were so sorry to part, and almost discouraged to try and go any farther, but we thought we would try our best any way to help him. We were only going to take a cup each and a little tea pail. No blanket. Found too weak to carry anything, but Mr. Hubbard made us take a part of a blanket each. We only had two pair blankets. My blanket I had left behind a few days ago.

So Mr. Hubbard told Mr. Wallace, "If you don't want to tear your blankets, you can tear my blankets in half, and each have a piece. It will be only one and half pound each to carry. Then I can use your blankets while you're away."

Then we tore Mr. Hubbard's blankets, and Wallace and I took each a piece. Also he made us take the rest of the pea meal and little tea. We left him little tea and the bones and piece of flour bag we found, with little mouldy lumps of flour sticking to the bag, and the neighbour of the other moccasin we had eaten.

Mr. Hubbard said, "After you go I will do some writing and will write a letter to Mrs. Hubbard."

Mr. Hubbard took his pistol off from his belt and gave me to take along. He also handed me his knife and told me to leave the crooked knife I had to him. I didn't want to take his pistol. I was thinking about a pistol too. I thought when Wallace and I parted I could ask him for his pistol; but Mr. Hubbard told me, "You must take the pistol. The rifle will be here, and I can use the rifle if I have anything to shoot. You must take the pistol."

So I took the pistol; but the knife I did not take.

Just before starting Mr. Wallace says that he is going to read a chapter before starting. Mr. Hubbard asked him to read the thirteenth chapter First Corinthians, and so he did.

It was time to start.

Mr. Wallace went to Mr. Hubbard and said, "Good-bye, I'll try and come back soon."

Then I went to him and tried to be as brave as Wallace.

When I took his hand he said, "God bless you, George," and held my hand for some time.

I said, "The Lord help us, Hubbard. With His help I save you if I can get out." Then I cried like a child.

Hubbard said, "If it was your father, George, you couldn't try harder to save."

Wallace came back to Hubbard again, and cried like a child and kissed him; and again I went to him and kissed him and he kissed me, and said again, "The Lord help you, George."

He was then so weak that be could hardly speak.

We came away.

TRYING TO GET HELP

When we left Mr. Hubbard an east and raw wind was blowing, and soon rain began, and heavy rain all way, and were soaked to the skin, and made poor time. We followed the river as it ran out into Grand Lake. The least thing we tripped on we would fall, and it would be some time before we could get up. Or we went too near a tree, that a branch would catch on us, would pull us down. At dark we stopped for the night. The trees were very small, and we couldn't get any shelter at all, and hard to get wood with no axe. We pulled together some half rotten lain trees. Our fire wouldn't burn hardly, and couldn't dry our things, and had to sit up all night with wet clothes on, near our fire, or rather near our smoke, as the wood being too rotten that it wouldn't burn. About two o'clock the wind turned westward, the rain ceased, but it began to snow very hard. The night was long and my mind on Hubbard all the time could not forget him.

In the morning, Monday, Oct. 19th, the snow nearly up to our knees. We started early. Our eyes were quite dim with the smoke and everything looked blue. It troubled us all day. Before noon I tracked up a partridge. Oh, how I wished to get him! I came to the place where he had flown away and hunted for him quite a while. At last he flew off. I was just near him and yet did not see him, about 4 feet over my head; but I saw where he perched. I didn't want to go too near him for fear he might fly away before I could shoot him. I was so particular. I rested my pistol on a tree to make a sure shot, and took a good aim, but only scraped him, and he nearly fell too, but after all got off. I cannot tell how sorry I was; and about noon we had to cross this river because the flour was on the opposite side. It was quite a rapid and I knew farther down that we could not get across, as I remembered from this rapid to where the flour is, it was deep. So we went into the cold, icy water up to our waists. We got across and made a fire, and had a cup of tea. It was yet a long way from the flour. We started off as soon as we could. It cleared up in the afternoon, and only drifting and freezing very hard, was getting colder and colder towards evening. Mr. Wallace I knew was near his finish; but I would not say or ask him about it. I thought I would scare him, and he would scare me too if he told me he could not go any further. I was getting so very, very weak myself.

The sun was getting low and I could yet walk lots faster than Wallace, and had to stand and wait for him very often, though I could hardly walk myself. I thought this was my last day that I could walk. If I don't come to the flour this evening I fear I will not be able to walk in the morning; and if I get to where the flour is, and the mice or some animal has carried it off it will surely mean death. And besides I wanted to know very, very much if the flour was there.

Just near dusk, Mr. Wallace was so much behind I thought I would tell him to follow my trail and he could come along behind, and I would try and get to the flour before dark. I stayed and waited till he came near.

He asked me, "How far yet to the flour?"

"About 2 miles," I said.

"Well I think you had better go along and not wait for me any more. I will try and follow your trail. You go lots faster than I do. Go on while it is yet light, and see if you can find the flour; because if you cannot get there to-night may be you will not be able to go any farther should we live to see morning."

I said, "Yes, that is just what I was going to tell you, the reason why I waited here for you."

I started off. I went about 40 yards. Came across a partridge. I got my pistol and fired and killed him. Oh, how glad I was! Mr. Wallace came to me. He was more than glad, and just ate part of him raw, which freshened us up a great deal.

Then he said, "You can go on again and don't delay on me."

I came on some caribou trail (it was then getting dark) and quite fresh, which run in all directions. I stood and thought, "When Wallace comes here he will not know my trail from the caribou trail; and if he cannot come to me to-night, if he follow the caribou trail it might lead him out of the way altogether; and if it snows again to-night I may not be able to find him in the morning."

So I stayed till he came and told him why I waited for him. He was glad and said sure he would not know my trail from the caribou, which would perhaps lead him out of the way. So we sat down and ate some more of the partridge raw.

Mr. Wallace says, "I just fancy that I never ate something so good in my life."

We could have camped right there where I killed the partridge, as we would have something for our supper; but what I wanted to find out too was—Is the flour there I wonder. If we did not get there it would be in my mind all the time, "I wonder if the flour is there." It got dark and we still travelled. Wallace would often ask me, "How far is it from here to the flour?" "How far is it to the flour?"

At last I knew we were coming to it. We had not a mark, or never put it at some particular place; but we have just thrown it away. Anyway we thought we would never come past there again. It was late in the night when we came to the flour. I was not very sure of it myself. I put down my little load.

Wallace said, "Is this the place?"

I said, "Yes."

So I went to where I thought we had left the flour. I dug down into the snow and just came on it. It was, of course, in one solid lump and black with mould. We got our knife and broke it off in bits and ate quite a bit. We were just about played out when we came to the flour. If I hadn't killed the partridge we would never have got to the flour.

We gathered some wood and made a fire. No trees at all so as to break the wind. All barren and the wind sharp, and clear night. We gathered enough wood for the night, and had the rest of the partridge, and also some flour soup in our little tea pail, and only wishing Mr. Hubbard was with us to enjoy the meal too. We thought and talked about Mr. Hubbard all the time, although at the same time having poor hopes of him. Mr. Wallace nearly blind and suffering with his eyes.

I sat up all night and kept on a fire. I was very uneasy about Wallace and afraid he would not be able to go back to Mr. Hubbard with the flour; but in the morning he was better and we did some patching on our old moccasins. We had some flour soup. Last night I did not notice in the dark the colour of our soup, till this morning when we had our breakfast about daylight. It was just black with the mouldy flour; but we found it very good. Nothing was too bad for us to eat. We were feeling good and fresh in the morning and expecting to make good time in travelling. I took my share of the flour, about two pounds, and gave Mr. Wallace about six or seven pounds, stuck fast on the bag. He told me to take more, but I would not take any more. I said, "I will trust in getting some game," as I would get to the wood country soon.

Before we parted I read the Sixty-seventh Psalm—

"God be merciful unto us and bless us, and cause his face to shine upon us. "That thy way may be known upon the earth, thy saving health among all nations. "Let the people praise thee, O God; let all the people praise thee. "O let the nations be glad and sing for joy; for thou shalt judge the people righteously, and govern the nations upon earth. "Let the people praise thee, O God; let all the people praise thee.

"Then shall the earth yield her increase: and God even our God shall bless us. "God shall bless us: and all the ends of the earth shall fear him."

Then I read a Thanksgiving Prayer:

"Almighty God, Father of all Mercies, we Thine unworthy servants do give Thee most humble and hearty thanks for all Thy goodness and loving-kindness to us and to all men. We bless Thee for our creation and preservation and all the blessings of this life; but above all for Thine inestimable love in the redemption of the world by our Lord Jesus Christ; for the means of grace and for the hope of glory. And we beseech Thee give us that due sense of all Thy mercies, that our hearts may be unfeignedly thankful and that we shew forth Thy praise not only with our lips, but in our lives, by giving up ourselves to Thy service and by walking before Thee in holiness and righteousness all our days, through Jesus Christ our Lord. To Whom with Thee and the Holy Ghost be all honour and glory world without end. Amen."

Then I told him what to do, for him not to leave the river, but to follow the river. I was afraid he might some time leave the river and wouldn't be able to find the river again, and lose his way. And if he gets to Hubbard and Hubbard yet alive, "if he gets little stronger by this flour, should he wish to come on, do the same, follow the river near, all the time; because if I happen to get down safe, and if I am too weak to come up myself when I send up help I shall tell them which side of the river to follow and they will surely meet you."

We found sorry to part, not knowing if we would meet again; but we must try and help Hubbard and do all we can for him. Wallace starts off on our back trail and I started toward Grand Lake. We said, "Good-bye, and 'God be with you till we meet again,'" to each other. We parted on a barren hill and could see each other for some time. We would just walk a few yards and sing out to each other, "Good-bye." This we kept on till out of sight and some distance apart.

It snowed very hard all day, and couldn't hardly see any distance. In the afternoon I killed a porcupine. How I wished I could give some to the boys.

Wednesday, 21st, had snowed heavy all night, and made heavy travelling without snowshoes, and the snow above my knees. To-day I saw a caribou and got a shot at him with my pistol. In the evening I killed another porcupine. I thought, "I shall be able to get out to Grand Lake now if the snow don't get too deep for me."

ThursdaY, 22nd. Snowing very hard again and cold. I made a fire at noon and tried to patch my shoe-packs but I couldn't spare time. I walked with only my socks, on in the afternoon and made poor time, as the country very rough and the snow very deep. I tried to make a straight road to make it short to Grand Lake. During the day though feeling very tired and would like to have a rest, if I stopped even for five minutes, lots Of things would come into my mind, and would have to start on again. At night it isn't so bad, because I try to make myself believe because it is night therefore I cannot travel."

Friday, 23rd, more snow again. In the afternoon got mild, and being so much snow on the trees, it began to drop. It was worse than any rain and the bush so thick to go through, and at last it began to rain. I was soaked to the skin, and the snow very deep. My hands were always so cold without mits, and travelling in such a rough country, and falling down often into the snow and rocks, and cutting my hands on the rocks. I at last cut part off the sleeves off my undershirt and with a string tied one end, and I slipped them on my hands for mits. Several times that day I had the notion of giving up, as I could not get on at all in the deep snow. I thought it was impossible to get through. Then again I would try and make my way out. I came to the place where we had left the coffee and milk. I found the coffee. The lid was off and the can was full of ice. I took the ice out and underneath of the ice the coffee was. I broke some off and made some coffee; but it did not hardly taste like coffee at all, all the strength was out, as it had been in water for a short time. The milk I could not find.

That evening I killed four partridges. The weather turned clear and cold and I was wet to the skin. It was late when I had to stop for the night, and did my best in trying to dry my things the best way I could, and hard to get wood for I had no axe.

Saturday, 24th, in the evening I came to the place where we had left the lard. I was very glad to find it. It was about three pounds of lard in a pail. I had some porcupine and a few partridges yet, as I would try and save some ahead for my way out, and the bones of the porcupine I carried with me; for I didn't throw the bones away, as it will make good broth if I get out of grub and don't get more game. I also had the flour yet, because I was saving it when my porcupine was done, and the porcupine bones with little flour will last me for a while. In the evenings I would talk to myself like as if some one with me, and plan to start off again soon as daylight, and try and make so many miles, just to cheer myself.

After I left Mr. Wallace, when coming along after I killed the porcupine and some partridges, at night, my fire I would have it in a long style and just lie near the side of it, and whatever I had, some porcupine or partridge, in my little bundle, I would put it for my pillow for fear some animal might carry it away. My pistol I would keep it handy, and then talk to myself and say, "If some wolves should come along to-night they would make short work of me. But I guess I might just as well get killed by them as to starve; but any way I will just make that first fellow jump a little with my pistol. My little pistol is only 22 cal."

Every evening I always read a chapter, and every morning at just break of daylight; and when I got a little stronger, after getting some game, strong enough to raise my voice, I always sung a part of a hymn. In the evening I would read first then sing,

"Lead kindly light, amid the encircling gloom
Lead Thou me on.
The night is dark, and I am far from home;
Lead Thou me on.
Keep Thou my feet; I do not ask to see
The distant scene; one step enough for me."

And in the morning after I read, I would sing,

Come to me, Lord, when first I wake,
As the faint lights of morning break;
Bid purest thoughts within me rise,
Like crystal dew-drops to the skies.

Sunday, 25th, was snowing again. In the evening I killed four more partridges. Snow very deep and made poor time, and high mountains to go over, but I thought I will get out to Grand Lake early in the morning.

Monday, 26th, I got out to Grand Lake about 10 o'clock and was very, very glad to get out again to the lake, but was very much disappointed in the afternoon. I came along the south shore of the lake and thinking I would make good time from there now to Northwest River, and I would only follow the shore of the lake to Northwest River, and besides no mountains to go over. I went about 2 miles and came to a river, which made me feel very bad about it, and I did not know how I could ever get across, and could not make a raft without an axe. I thought I would try any way to make a raft, if I could only get wood to make a raft with. I followed the river up. The banks were so high, and the swift current run so swift along the steep banks, and the river very deep. I could not drop a log in without it float right away, and also came to another branch. This river branches off in two. I tried all afternoon to cross at the main river so I would have only one river to cross; but I could not there, as near the lake I will have two rivers to cross at the forks.

I gave up and went down near the lake again. The ice was floating down the river. A rapid near the lake. I thought it might not be very deep. Then, seeing that I could not do any better, I thought I would wade out a piece and the rest I would swim to the other shore.

I started out, and up to my waist before I got any distance out, and the floating ice coming against me, and the cramps began to take on the legs, that I was obliged to turn and just got out to shore in time.

I stood for some time thinking that I will never be able to cross, and that I would sure to starve there. It got dusk and I started a fire. I was very, very cold, and had something to eat. I was troubled very much and could not forget the river, and the ice floating and rubbing against the shore, made things worse, to hear that sound all night, and thinking if I only had a canoe, I could get to Northwest River to-morrow. It was yet 40 miles to the post Northwest River.

Tuesday, 27th, as soon as daylight I tried to wade across again the same place; but things happened the same. Along the lake lots of drift wood. I thought I better make a raft if I could. It was blowing very heavy from the west. I got my raft made. My tump line I made two pieces to tie the four corners of the raft, and my leather belt I made another piece, and a piece of small salmon twine I had at the other corner. I got a long pole so as to be sure and touch bottom with it all the way across, as I was afraid that the swift current would take me out into the lake and the heavy sea would swamp me.

My raft was too small, and when I got on it I sunk down quite a bit. I shoved out and came to the strong current, and the tide and the ice overcame me, and took me out to the lake. When the current took me out into the lake, then the wind caught me and carried me. It got so deep I could not find bottom with my pole. I had a mind to jump from the raft; but I knew if I did I would surely get drowned. So I thought I might just as well try to stay on. My raft was breaking up. Piece by piece would float away. So I got down on my knees and tried to keep the pieces together, and the sea would just cover me. For about two hours I stayed on the raft, and sure it was my finish. Finally, after a while, the wind drove me just near a point. It was a long point, and I knew I could touch bottom with my pole. I took my pole and just hardly got ashore. (Grand Lake runs nearly east and west, is over 40 miles long, and from 1 to 4 miles wide, and very deep, up to sixty fathom of water, and for the least wind makes a very heavy sea.)

At this point where I got ashore, I was more than glad, but the other branch yet to cross. I came to the branch and followed it up quite a bit. This branch is much larger than the first. It was very hard to get wood to make a raft. No drift. I managed to shove some half rotten stumps down. It took me some time to get enough for my raft, and not a stitch dry about me, just wringing wet, and would not make a fire till I got across the other branch. I built my raft on newly frozen ice, just near the open stream, and then broke the ice around and with a long pole worked my way across. This raft was much larger than the first, and out of the water where I stood. Oh! but I was so proud of that raft, and talking to myself all the time, and telling myself what a fine raft it was, and I was so proud of my raft. I got across safe and without much trouble after all.

It was nearly sunset. I thought I'd better make my fire and found I was nearly safe. I would dry up and make a good early start in the morning, and would nearly get to the post the next day. I picked out a place for the night, and shot three partridges right there. It was near a point where I was and round the point run a deep bay. I thought may be another river run out from there. And just to see if I could see any river I run to the point. When I got to the point, I seeing a small boat within 100 yards from me; and, of course, to make sure, I run to see it, thinking it would come handy to me and I could sail to the post.

Before I came near it, a child screamed out nearly opposite of me in the bush. I cannot tell how I felt. I just run the direction I heard the sound. The next, the roof of a house I saw. Then I came on a trail. I saw a girl with a child outside of the door. As soon as she saw me she run in and a woman came out. I sung out to her before I came to her. Meeting me she looked so scared. Then I shook hands with her, and told her where I came from. She took me in the house and told me to sit down. But I was—well I could not say how I was and how glad I was.

After I had some tea and bread, I went for my little bundle and the partridges I shot. When I got back, a bed was fixed up for me and a shift of dry clothes. She did not know what to think of me when first seeing me, and also being all wet and nearly barefooted. She was the wife of Donald Blake.

When I came there at Donald's I had six partridges, and a piece of porcupine and about half of the flour I started off with, and all the bones of the porcupine that I carried along with me.

145

TOO LATE

Very soon Donald Blake and his brother came home. I told him of our sad trip, and asked him if he could go up and take grub to Mr. Hubbard and Wallace.

"Which river did you follow this summer?" Donald asks me.

"The Nascaupee River," I said, "and I came down by the same river again."

"When did you come out to Grand Lake?" he said.

"Yesterday," I replied.

"And how did you get across the lake?

"I did not come across at all, but I followed the south shore all the way."

Then he told me where the Nascaupee River was, and where it came out from to the Grand Lake within 4 miles northeast from here. I told him about which river we followed, the one at the head of the lake. He then tells me that we have taken the wrong river, and that the river we have followed was the Susan River.

Then I asked him, "What river was this one I crossed with the raft?"

He says, "That river was Beaver Brook or Beaver River."

Then I learnt that this Beaver River was the Big River where we left our canoe, and my thoughts were, "Oh! that if we had followed the Big River, we would have all got out safe," and I could not forget about it, and felt so sorry about it.

Donald got ready to start in the morning. He told me of two men 7 miles from here. I told him it would be better if we could get the other two men, as they would make better time and have lighter loads. So they started off the same night in their boat, and got the two men, Allan Goudy and Duncan M'Lean.

Wednesday morning, October 28th.—Donald and three more started off in their boat part of the way. They had their snowshoes also. Taking lots of grub and some spare sealskin boots and some other clothes, as I told them how the boys were rigged when I left them. I wanted to go with them too; but they said they were going to travel at night too, and thought I would not be able to stand it out. I made a map for them and told them just where the tent was, and told them which side of the river to follow, and that the tent was just at the forks. I told them what I told Wallace before I left him, not to leave the river and to follow the north shore of the river all the time. So they said they would find the camp without any trouble.

When Donald and the men had gone, Mrs. Blake was baking some biscuits just after breakfast. The hot biscuits looked so good. At last, I could not help myself, and had to ask her for some. She put some in a dish and gave me butter, molasses, and tea. So I ate and ate, and could not stop myself whatever, that at last I had to just force myself to go away where I could not see those little biscuits.

But oh! how I did suffer afterwards. I could not eat any thing more that day. It pained me ever so much in my breast. I would try and have a rest in bed, but could not, the pain was too much. Then I would go out and walk about outside; but it was no use whatever, and come in and sit down. This I kept on all day but I wouldn't tell Mrs. Blake about it. I had no rest and suffered very much and was getting worse all the time. I thought of myself: Well I had nearly died of starvation, and after I did come out to where I could get some grub to live on, and after all kill myself with it. What a mean trick.

I did not know what to do with myself at last. Then I thought to try some hot water and started to vomit. It did me good. I felt much better after. I knew when I was eating those biscuits, that it wouldn't be good for me if I ate too much, but I couldn't help it. But it learnt me a good lesson. Afterwards I took good care not to eat too much. But for some time after, about three weeks, we suffered in our breast every time we ate, and so very, very hungry all the time for more to eat. We then suffered nearly as much as we did when we were first out of grub.

Next day Mrs. Blake telling me, "Donald built this house this fall. It is a little over a week since we moved into our new house. And the other house you see over there is Mr. Bakie's house. He is not up yet. He is yet at the Northwest River post."

So I thought, "If Donald hadn't come up here when I came past!!!—I guess I will just go into Mr. Bakie's house and see if I would have found any thing there."

I went in his little store first, it wasn't locked, and found a few pounds of flour and some bits of pork in a keg, and about twenty pounds butter and also a good pair of sealskin boots.

So I said to myself, "Well, I guess I could find a load of grub here and take a load back to Mr. Hubbard and Wallace."

But I thought about the river, and how would I get a load back across the river? Then I looked round if I could find an axe, and found two, one small and the other large.

I took the big axe and said, "This one would come handy to use to make my raft with, and the little one I would take along with me in the bush, and those sealskin boots I would wear."

And also found three pair snowshoes. I also picked out the pair I would have taken and said, "This pair I would take."

Then I went in his house and found two barrels of flour.

So I said, "Well, after all I would have found more flour than I could carry to take up to the boys," for I told them when I left, that if I found grub any place on the road, and no one there, I will just help myself and try and bring up a load. In that house I spent some time, thinking and planning of what I would have done.

Friday, October 30th.—I was staying at Donald's, killing quite a few partridges and making myself at home; but yet not feeling very happy, as I did not get much rest at nights, thinking about Mr. Hubbard and anxious to hear from them soon. I had good hopes of Mr. Wallace, because the mouldy flour he had would yet keep him alive. And my troubles were: "Now I feel safe and in good hopes of getting home; but should Mr. Hubbard and Wallace starve in there, the people may not believe me in what I say, and will think that I run away from them, and haven't done fair whatever," and when I got home I would get in trouble, after I had done all I could for them as well as myself.

When I would wake up at night it would just come into my mind. And more than that, Mr. Hubbard had been so good to me, and to remember what a friend he was, and what a brave man he was. Oh! wasn't he a brave man. I have seen a good many fine people in my time; but I never have seen a man like Hubbard, and I never expect to see another.

I was thinking too how things happened, about being on the wrong river, and what made us believe we were on the right river, though at the same time thinking that it was too small to feed Grand Lake, but when it came out just at the head of the lake, as it shows in the map, made us think it was the Nascaupee. And besides how we proved as we were going up, as the people had told us at Northwest River post, that after we got up the Nascaupee River, 18 miles up, we would come to the Red Wine River, branching off from the south side of the Nascaupee River, and also how that happened. When we got up, about 18 miles up, a little river branching off from the south into this river we thought was the Nascaupee, and of course, we called this little river the Red Wine River. And besides how we found the old portage trail, and also the steel trap, and how all these things kept on making us think for sure we were on the right route. And besides none knew, or ever thought, there was any other river. And I could not forget about it, and was so sorry about it. Only one river.

Saturday evening, October 31st.—Donald Blake and Allan Goudy returned from their trip, and sorry to hear the death of Mr. Hubbard. They suppose he died the first evening we left him, by telling of the signs, as he hasn't been out of the tent after the first snow. Three or four caribou has been coming right near the tent door, and going round the tent.

148

Donald and Allan tells of Mr. Hubbard and how they had found him wrapped up in his blanket, like as he had been falling asleep, and the tent door closed and all pinned up. I could tell then pretty well how he has being, and that be has being doing as he said he would, and has fallen asleep and has never woke. For I myself was nearly at my finish, and knew how I felt, and how weak and sleepy I used to feel, and often felt that I could just fall asleep and never wake up again.

Donald and Allan brought all that was at the tent, Mr. Hubbard's camera and his rifle and his diary. And I was so very much surprised to see what he has written, and found a letter he has been writing for me to Mr. S. A. King, in case I should fail, and telling him how I had tried so hard to help him. I was so glad to see this letter, and remembered how he did speak of me this summer, and was so always pleased of my work. And further, to see here what he has written about me, even to his very last.

Then I knew his letter would help if the people would not believe me in what I said.

They fixed Mr. Hubbard's body the best way they could and returned to Mr. Wallace. Going up they found Mr. Wallace 1 mile above from where we got the flour from, where Wallace and I parted. They came on to his trail first. Then they followed him up. He has crossed the river on the ice to the south shore, just near where they came to him along the river, where some caribou had been going across. He had a little fire, but was unable to make a start or to travel any more. Allan Goudy says he right away gave Wallace some bread and butter, and after he ate that he did want some more: "But we would not give him more. We were afraid to give him too much, for fear he would eat too much. He then got a hold of some raw salt pork and was going to eat it raw, that we had just to take it from him."

The two young lads, Duncan M'Lean and Gilbert Blake, stayed with Mr. Wallace, and Donald and Allan went right on to Mr. Hubbard. They saw Wallace's trail through the snow, and along where he went, and only less than a couple hundred yards from the tent, and had turned back and followed his own trail again, thinking he had gone past the camp. They found Mr. Wallace was frost-bitten on the point of his toe, the big toe on his left foot. He had yet a little of the flour when they found him. The two lads stays up with Mr. Wallace, so when he gets a little stronger they would come down to Grand Lake. They had a tent and stove, and lots of provisions.

Sunday, November 1st.—I went with Allan over where be lives, 7 miles from Donald's, 4 miles by the lake, then up the Nascaupee River 3 miles. My first glimpse of the Nascaupee River. The Nascaupee River is a nice big river compared to the Susan and Beaver River, and much wider and deeper. When we came along here in the summer, we saw this bay where the Nascaupee River comes out from, from a distance; but we thought it was just only a bay, and high mountains all round, and we never thought a river came out from there. So we did not go in there at all. We saw also from a distance, where Beaver River run out from; but we thought it was only an island. So we still just went on and followed the map.

It was late in the evening when we got back to Donald's. Donald and Allan would start off again in the morning to meet the two lads and Wallace.

Monday, November 2nd.—Donald and Allan meeting Mr. Wallace, they arrived at Donald's in the evening. Mr. Wallace then told me of his trip after I left him; but he couldn't remember all, as he at last lost track of every thing. He was troubled with his eyes, being nearly smoke blind, and that he could not find the tent. He thought he had gone past the camp. He says he did not know where the tent was. He made Duncan a present of Mr. Hubbard's washing rod.

Tuesday, November 3rd.—We said good-bye to Donald's, and went with Allan and Duncan over to their place. We staid there couple of days while Allan getting his boat ready for us to use to Northwest River. The day after I went over there I asked Duncan M'Lean if he could go with me this winter when I go up to get Mr. Hubbard's body. He told me he would be willing to come along with me and help me all he could. I told him I would try to get one or two more at Northwest River post.

Thursday, Noveinber 5th.—In the morning Wallace and I started off from Allan's house. When we got to the mouth of the river we could not go any farther. Snowing very hard and could not see any distance, and the wind against us. We stayed at the mouth of the river till in the evening. The wind shifted to the northwest, and we sailed across to Cape Blanc, just opposite the Nascaupee. We went to a little shack I knew. When we passed here in the summer we saw the shack just near the lake. This was the little shack where I thought I might find some food or, perhaps, find some trappers when I was coming down the Susan; but it was just a little shack or tilt for the trappers' use when travelling along Grand Lake, just big enough for two men to sleep in. Wallace and I were glad to get in, and a little stove in too, and nice and warm.

In the morning, Nov. 6th, nice wind and fair for us, and got to Northwest River. The people were so sorry to hear the sad news of Mr. Hubbard, especially those who have seen him.

I also came across Mr. Bakie, who knew about Beaver River, and enquires if we came to where it branches and connects again, on the south side of a high half barren hill.

I said, "Yes, that is just the place where we left our canoes and went over to Susan Brook."

He tells me, "If you had come over that rapid where you left the canoe, you would go 6 miles and just come to another. Only about 50 yards you would carry your canoe, and from there smooth and deep water, no rapids, but swift current. Even if you didn't have the strength of paddling, the swift current would have brought you down, right down to my house."

Mr. Bakie lives just near Donald Blake's at Grand Lake, just near the river—Beaver River. How sorry I was when we did not follow Beaver River. It would only take us two days to come from where we left the canoe to where Donald Blake or Mr. Bakie's house. Mr. Bakie has his trapping on Beaver River, and he knew all about it, and tells me that we had come over the worst part of the river.

KEEPING A PROMISE AND SOMETHING MORE

At the New Year I saw Duncan M'Lean again, and he said he would meet me on the 16th January at Donald's, to start from there up the bush to get Mr. Hubbard's body, and the things we left, if I can find them. He would be out from his trapping path then, and besides the rivers frozen up. All the people round there thought that I could not find anything whatever.

I did not meet Duncan, and did not get started on my trip till 8th March. The men were willing to go with me and help me with what I had to do; but Mr. Wallace wanted the canoe out, and to make the canoe a present to Mr. M'Kenzie, which the boys didn't care to undertake, and afraid to try and make a start, because they thought if they went they would have to bring the canoe. And besides the snow being so deep, and had been snowing nearly every day for some time ago, and haven't had chance of settling down, and besides about 80 miles to where the camp was, and the canoe about 98 miles. We could not take dogs, because the country being so rough we could not use dogs whatever. So we have to get on by hauling every man his toboggan.

Seeing that the boys were almost afraid to try, till at last I told them, "Never mind, but come along with me and I will tell you whether the canoe will be taken out or not. Because we are going up there especially for to bring out Mr. Hubbard's body, and some films if I can find them, and we will leave the canoe and not bother with it. So you can put the blame on me, as anyway we will have more than three men can handle, and especially the country being so rough."

They said they would come along with me and help me in what I had to do, as it is something that has to be done. And besides getting time for the mild, and the rivers burst, and the water runs on top of the ice, and afraid that we could do no travelling in Susan Brook, and the mountains so rough and steep we could not haul toboggans over them, and have to travel on the river. So we got started in the morning from Northwest River on our way up.

March 8th.—Tom Blake and Duncan M'Lean and I started this morning to bring Mr. Hubbard's body out to Northwest River. We have two toboggans and one catmeran. Taking little stove, and tent and enough provisions. Each has a good load, and the new snow makes heavy going. Got dogs at Tom Blake's. Douglas Blake going up the lake with us. We came 18 miles to-day.

March 9th.—Still snowing heavy and stormy. So we had to lay up to-day, being too rough to travel on the lake, and the snow deep.

March 10th.—Still snowing. Tom Blake got discouraged, as he thinks it will be too hard to do any travelling in the bush, as it is heavy going even on the lake. He and Douglas went home this morning with the dogs to Northwest River. The young lad Duncan stays with me. I found hard to think of what I have to do; but Duncan promises me that he will be brave, and we will try and go on as soon as the weather settles, and the snow will pack and make better travelling.

March 11th and 12th.—Snowing and kind of mist. Could not go on again.

Sunday, March 13th.—In the afternoon it cleared up and we started, Duncan and I, and being only two could not take all we had, and left some grub and our blankets. Just taking tent, stove, and enough grub. Our loads still heavy to drag, and travelled slow and good part of the night. At last Duncan broke his snowshoe, and had to stop. Duncan is a nice boy and willing, and not particular when to start in the morning and when to quit.

March 14th.—This morning Duncan fixing up his snowshoes, and took part of the day. In the afternoon we started. Hope to make a good early start in the morning as the snow is settling fast.

March 15th.—This morning, as we were just starting off, saw Mr. Blake coming. He has changed his mind and came on again to follow us up. We were so glad to have him come again.

March 16th.—Stormy and cold. Last night very cold. We have to keep fire on all night, and especially when we have no blankets. Our toboggans being so rimey to-day, and very often scraped the rime off so as it wouldn't draw so hard.

March 17th.—The weather changed and settled down, and made a good day's journey to-day.

March 18th.—To-day I shot six partridges with the pistol. This evening I knew we were coming opposite where we left the cartridges in the summer. It was in July, when one day Mr. Hubbard thought he had too many cartridges, and we took and dug in the sand and left them and covered them up, about five hundred rifle and pistol cartridges. So I told Mr. Blake and Duncan about it, and left our loads there and crossed over to where I thought it would be. We hadn't marked the place, for any way we thought of never coming back that way again. We came to the place where I thought we had left them, and dug into the snow. The boys were not sure about it at all, and thinking that I would not find the cartridges.

When we came to the sand they asked me, "Is this the place?"

I said, "Yes."

A chisel I had with me to cut the frozen sand with. We dug into the sand and just came on them. The boys were surprised and would have bet anything before we started that I wouldn't find anything whatever, as the snow in winter makes things look different.

March 19th.—To-day made good time. Duncan snow blind.

Sunday, March 20th.—Early before noon we came to the camp. The tent was all buried in the snow; but when we dug down were surprised to find it standing. We wrapped Mr. Hubbard in the things we brought along with us, and did the best we could.

I blazed a tree near where the tent has been. This I wrote deeply:

L. HUBBARD
died here 18th October, 1903, and
will be brought out by
T. BLAKE, DUNCAN M'LEAN and G. ELSON.

Came on a little farther this evening. The boys yet do not hardly think I can find the rest of the things. Of course, I'm not sure myself; but I can try any way. We have our cache five different places, some 4 and 8 miles apart.

March 21st.—The boys were surprised to-day. When we came to the first cache I told them that we left some things there; but they looked at me and told me, how could I tell and no marks to go by. But they wouldn't refuse. We dug down to the ground, 8 feet, and just came on our little bundle we had left. The next was the same, and the next, till we got everything we had thrown away, only one bag yet with lots of films in. I remembered that I had hung it up by a little strap, on a little stump in some swamp, and the trees scattered. I thought I really could not guess at that place, and told the boys; but we went on any way, till I thought we came to the place. No tree near, only just a plain. At last we dug down a piece any way. When we got down a piece we started to feel around with our feet, and just came on the stump, and the bag still on.

Mr. Blake says, "I have been trapping now ever since I could, when only a boy, and I think I know a little about travelling in the bush now; but I could never find anything like you, and did not miss one place, but came right on it every time. I would never believe any one could do that if I did not see it myself."

Duncan said the same, and besides nothing to go by.

March 22nd.—Started back from the camp for Grand Lake. Each man has a big load, for we have picked up lots. Duncan very bad with snow blind.

March 23rd.—Snowing heavy, and rime on our to boggans makes heavy travelling. Some places the river bad to travel, on account of rapids where it isn't froze. We have some times just a narrow bridge of ice to go on, as no other way we could go, for the rough steep mountains on each side.

March 24th.—Drifting and snowing very hard. Only travelled part of the day. Got to Allan Goudy's house.

March 25th.—Snowing heavy. Got to Cape Corbeau. All very tired.

March 26th.—Stormy to-day and snowing very hard, and our toboggans so heavy we could not get on at all, and had to leave our loads and walk empty to the post. Late when we got here at Mr. Blake's house at the rapids, 3 miles from the post. Will get dog team in the morning and go back for our loads.

March 28th.—Duncan M'Lean and I took dog team up Grand Lake this morning and got here again this evening with Mr. Hubbard's body and the things we left behind in the fall. We dressed him the best we could and laid him in the coffin the men at Kenemish had made for him, till we are ready to start on around the coast.

When I was up in the bush, Mr. Wallace has a letter from Dr. Cluny Macpherson. As soon as he heard the sad news of Mr. Hubbard, he has started from Battle Harbor to come to Northwest River with his dog team to help us. When he got to Rigolette, Mr. Fraser has just been at Northwest River post, and told him we hadn't yet the body of Mr. Hubbard out from the bush, and besides when he left Battle Harbor his little child was sick, and a team of dogs brought him news that his child was getting worse. So then he had to turn back from Rigolette, and sent a letter to Mr. Wallace to guide us on our way, from Rigolette to Battle Harbor, from the time we may leave Rigolette all along, giving full account where we could get men and teams, and when we got at a place what man to ask for, and gave all the names of the places, and the names of the people we are to enquire for, and the best places to stay at nights, and besides tells of a steamer to come to Battle Harbor about the first of May.

It was hard to get dogs and we were long getting started. In February I was up at Muddy Lake. Wednesday, Feb. 24th, I went from Muddy Lake to Goose Bay at John Groves. He asked me if we got dogs to help us around the coast and to take Mr. Hubbard's body. I said that we did not yet find teams that could take us around or even as far as Rigolette.

Thursday, February 25th.—I got to Northwest River.

Sunday, February 28th.—Mr. Wallace and Mr. Bently arrived from Kenemish. Then I told Mr. Wallace what John Groves had told me, that he could help us with his team as far as Rigolette any way, and that he had a good team of dogs.

Friday, April 8th.—Lots of teams from Muddy Lake. Edward Michline also arrived. He has been at Goose Bay a few days ago, and tells me that his brother-in-law John Groves said, that if Mr. Wallace would ask him to help him along, he could go as far as Rigolette with his team of dogs, as at the time he did not have very much to do and he could have time to go to Rigolette and back before he had any particular work to do for himself. Then I told Mr. Wallace about it, what John Groves has said. He said that he would write a letter to him and ask him about it.

But Mr. Wallace and Mr. M'Kenzie still thinking of getting the canoe out, and wanted me to go up the Grand Lake and up by Beaver Brook, to get the canoe out to Northwest River.

I was not careful of undertaking the trip. My reasons why—I knew how long it would take me to go up and back again to Northwest River. It would take me nearly two weeks. I thought it would be pretty late when we could make a start on our trip to Battle Harbor, and would miss the boat that Dr. Macpherson told us would be in Battle Harbor about the 1st of May. Also I was sure that the canoe would be crushed to pieces with the weight of the snow, as we left it in a place where it had a good chance of being crushed to the ground. If we had put it in some shelter where it would be all right, or if we had put it on a stage to keep in good shape; but when we had just taken it out of the river, and just left it along the open, I knew it could not be safe. I thought it was a piece of nonsense to try and get it out, and would be only a trip for nothing. Even then I would be willing to go if it hadn't been so late. Also I thought it was hardly fair to try and force me to go any way, because I knew that I wasn't under either of them. I was hired by Mr. Hubbard on the trip and we had to do all the planning. It was Mr. Hubbard's expedition, and we had to obey him and try to help him in all we could while we were yet together. Also Mr. Hubbard had done and has always left things in my care to which I thought it would be better for us to do, and has gone by my plans a good deal, though he was the head of the party. Also what was belonging to Mr. Hubbard, knowing that I had just as much rights with some of his things as any one had, and in fact that I had already done that would be required, and had gotten out everything that I thought was necessary to be gotten out from the bush. However at last I said that I would go if I got a dog team. So I got ready to start to go for the canoe.

Wallace told me, "You see, if when you went up, if you had dug up the canoe out of the snow and put it up on a stage, you wouldn't have to go up again."

I said, "I do not have to go up again. It is not long since I had my trip up there. I think I have done my part."

I was to start Tuesday, April 12th.

Monday, April 11th.—Mr. Wallace wrote a letter and wrote to John Groves telling him to be at Northwest River at such a day, about the time we would be out with the canoe from Grand Lake and Beaver River. Sent his letter up by Carl Hope.

Tuesday, April 12th.—A pile snowing and we could not go. Mark Blake and I were to start this morning but too stormy.

Wednesday, April 13th.—Still very stormy and lots of new snow has been falling, and could not make a start again. I told Wallace and M'Kenzie that if I could not go off again the next morning I would give up the trip and not go at all, as it was getting too late.

Thursday, April 14th.—Still stormy and snowing very hard, so that we could not go again, and gave up the trip.

Monday, April 18th.—Henry and his brother Dan Groves arrived. I told Mr. Wallace about them and that he could send word by them to tell their brother John Groves to come right away and help up to Rigolette.

Tuesday, April 19th.—John Groves arrived and said that he could not come along with us, as he had now lots of work that he wanted to do for himself, and besides his dogs were all cut by crust about the feet.

April 20th.—Getting ready for starting off in the morning. Getting help from M. Duclos, the French Company agent here. Sending his man Bellfleur to help me on to Rigolette with his dog team.

Thursday, April 21st.—Bellfleur and I started this morning from Northwest River with Mr. Hubbard's body. Starting a day ahead of Mr. M'Kenzie, as we have a heavy load and the going heavy. Will take three days to Rigolette. Mr. M'Kenzie will bring Wallace along with him and Fred Blake his teamster. They will overtake us on the way, as they have good dogs and no load only just themselves. Got to Lowlands at 10 o'clock to-night. Bad footing for our dogs, and had to lead them and break down the snow. We came 40 miles to-day and our dogs at last played out. Bob Bakie lives here and does his trapping around here. He tells us he killed a caribou to-day, a big stag.

April 22nd.—This morning gave our dogs a little rest, and did not start from Mr. Bakie's till noon. Our dogs are so poor that most of them are chaffed with the harness, and a mixed team, some water dogs, some Esquimaux dogs. The water dogs do not stand the hard work near so well as the huskies, and get played sooner. Before we started to-day one of the men killed four caribou there. Came here this evening at Bell Shepherd's.

Saturday evening, April 22rd.—Got to Rigolette. Mr. M'Kenzie caught up to us just a few miles before getting to Rigolette, and we got there together. Mr. Fraser, the agent at Rigolette, has some time ago been telling Jerry Flowers and his brother that we would be along at Rigolette, and asked them if they would help us along to Cartwright, and that he would let them know when we came to Rigolette.

Sunday, April 24th.—Mr. Fraser sent off two men to go and tell Jerry and his brother that we are at Rigolette.

Monday, April 25th.—Early this morning Jerry and brother came with team of dogs each, but they wouldn't go less than thirty dollars each for two days' run. Mr. Fraser told them they were charging too much and wouldn't have them, but got some other men for us. Left Rigolette in the afternoon. Crossed over river in a boat. Came to William Mugford's, 3 miles from Rigolette.

Tuesday, April 26th.—Snowing. Started at 6 A.M. Wind in our faces before noon and the new snow made heavy going. I have Mr. Hubbard's body on my sledge, and also some dunnage, and have four dogs. George Pottle my teamster. Wallace has George Williams for his teamster and six dogs. After noon the wind shifted to the northwest and the wind blew the snow off the crust, and fine going. A few ridges of hills we came over but not bad. Came 40 miles to-day. Came to Sam Pottle's house at West Bay at 6.30 P.M.

Wednesday, April 27th.—Started from West Bay 7 A.M. Got to Cartwright 4.30 P.M., 46 miles. Sam Pottle and George Williams our teamsters. Drifting and cold all day.

Thursday, April 28th.—Staying here at the post. Mr. Swaffield, agent here of the Hudson's Bay post, getting us another team. Only enough dogs for one team here. Mr. Swaffield has sent for Charles Davies to be ready for starting off in the morning.

Friday, April 29th.—This morning Mr. Davies took sick and was very bad. So Mr. Swaffield had to get us another man in his place, Walter Bird. Started 7 A.M. Got to Sandy Hill 2.30 P.M., and got so soft we could not travel, especially through the portages. Travelling mostly on ice. Came 30 miles.

Saturday, April 30th.—This morning we started from Sandy Hill 4 A.M., and got to Spotted Islands 8.30 A.M., 25 miles. Our teamsters don't know the route any farther. Mick Dison and Bill Dison our teamsters from Spotted Islands. Starting off in the afternoon 2.30 P.M., got to Seal Island 6 P.M., 20 miles.

Sunday, May 1st.—Very stormy and can't see any distance. Can't make a start to-day. Staying in George Morris house.

Monday, May 2nd.—Still stormy. We started from Seal Island, 11 A.M. after it cleared up a bit, and got to Coopers Bite, or New York, 7 P.M., 35 miles. Nobody living there. We came to some shacks. No stoves in any of them and all the doors off. We gathered some of the old broken stoves and made kind of a fireplace in the middle of the house, and built a fire. We cut a hole in the roof to let the smoke out.

Tuesday, May 3rd.—Started off this morning 4 A.M. It was yet dark. Got to Williams Harbor 9 A.M., 30 miles. Came to Mr. John Russel's house. Mr. Russel and his brother James Russel has been just starting off into the bay, and will not be home till evening. Mick and Bill Dison do not know the route an farther.—The Russels home this evening, and will take us to Fox Harbor in the morning.

Wednesday, May 4th.—Started off from Williams Harbor early this morning 6 A.M., and came to Mr. George Wakeham's at Fox Harbor about 10 A.M., 25 miles. Cannot get across the bay and the people tell us that we cannot go round by dog team, on account of a river near Cape Charles. So we have to wait here till the ice moves out. Only 6 miles from Battle Harbor. We stay here at Mr. Wakeham's. The people all along on our trip has been good to us as they could. We had only to go by Dr. Macpherson's letter, and at every place they were always ready to help us, because when the Dr. has passed he told them about us coming along the coast, and they were always looking out for us. The people all along the coast has heard of my finding the things on my trip in the bush. One would tell the other, "This is the man we heard of, when he found everything he dug for in the snow this winter."

Thursday, May 12th.—About noon a little boat came from Battle Harbor to Fox Harbor. The Dr. had heard that we were at Fox Harbor, and right away sent a little boat with five men to help us, and telling us about a steamer at Cape Charles. She will be starting for Newfoundland may be in the morning. Wallace and I were more than glad, and started right away from Fox Harbor. We were there eight days at Fox Harbor. We came through the floating ice and went round to Cape Charles. Went aboard the steamer and found out that the Captain was at Battle Harbor. So we came round and got to Battle Harbor late in the evening.

Friday, May 13th.—Dr. Macpherson had Mr. Hubbard's body enclosed in a lead coffin. In the afternoon we went aboard the steamer *Aurora*, Capt. Kean, that had gone to Cape Charles with a load of machinery for the new whale factory.

Saturday, May 14th.—In the evening, 7.30 P.M., and starting from Cape Charles for St. John's, Newfoundland.

Tuesday, May 17th.—Arrived at St. John's, Newfoundland.

Friday, May 27th.—Arrived at New York City.

Saturday, May 28th.—Mr. Hubbard's body was buried to-day in Mount Repose, in Haverstrawe.

Printed in Great Britain
by Amazon